This is not just a book about leadership or leadership development. It's an invitation to *discover* the authentic leader inside you. Whether you're in a formal leadership position or not, you've come to the right place. Let's get this journey started!

Jeremy

Jeremy Fyke, Ph.D.
www.AuthenticLeaderDevelopment.com

Praise for *Have We Met?*

This book is a treasure. Jeremy Fyke calls us to a growth mindset where we continue to learn and develop as leaders, emphasizing the importance of authenticity in all that we are and do. Both inspiring and practical, the book calls us forward to become far more than we are now and perhaps ever thought we could be. Take, read, enjoy, and grow!

–L. Gregory Jones, President, Belmont University

"With clear strategies and real-world examples, Dr. Fyke provides the roadmap for effective leadership. More than that, *Have We Met* is a hands-on resource that empowers you to lead with confidence, clarity, and purpose in line with who God created you to be. A game-changer for both new and seasoned leaders."

–Danny Gokey, award-winning Contemporary Christian Artist

Dr. Fyke delivers a clear, practical, and inspiring guide to help leaders unlock their full potential. His insights are both accessible and actionable, making this a must-read for anyone looking to grow, lead with impact, and drive meaningful results.

–Christine Belknap, Chief Human Resources Officer, TruGreen

Have We Met? provides a refreshing take on professional development. Complete with insightful stories and practical exercises, this book provides readers with the knowledge and tools they need to succeed. It is a game-changer for anyone whether you are a seasoned professional or just starting out.

–Laura Bagus, Chief Technology Officer, Vanderbilt University Medical Center

Dr. Fyke translates deep concepts into easy-to-read lessons in a way that challenges the reader to really take ownership of their development. *Have We Met?* is an insightful and practical guide that breaks down leadership development into clear, actionable steps. A must-read for anyone serious about growing as a leader.

–Kimberly Huffman, Vice President Human Resources, Banfield Pet Hospitals

This book provides refreshing and creative ways to focus on yourself while you focus on the many other demands of being a leader. The advice inside is relevant for anyone anywhere on their leadership journey–from those right out of college all the way up to the C-suite!

–Scott Corley, Vice President, Director of Athletics, Belmont University

Dr. Fyke's *Have We Met?* is a game-changer in LEADER development. Its blend of personal insights, research, and practical tools provides a unique and powerful approach for anyone serious about making a meaningful impact within their organization.

–Matthew Metzger, Vice President, Learning & Development, Dollar General Corporation

Have We Met? masterfully combines real-world experience, sharp insights, and practical strategies to deliver solutions that truly resonate. It's a must-read for anyone looking to deepen their understanding and take meaningful, lasting action. Dr. Fyke's unique blend of hands-on expertise and relatable examples creates an engaging, empowering guide for personal and professional growth. Whether you're seeking clarity, inspiration, or actionable tools, this book provides the perfect balance of wisdom and practicality to help you succeed!

–Phil Ellenburg, Chief Executive Officer,
Faith Family Medical Center

Clear, practical, and insightful advice for any leader looking to lead more effectively and authentically!

–Justin Nipper, Senior Vice President,
Chief Financial Officer, The Farmers Bank

Have We Met? is a must-read for anyone looking to elevate their leadership skills and become a more impactful leader. Dr. Fyke combines research-backed insights with real-world examples and actionable strategies into a guide that is both practical and personal. Whether you're an experienced leader or just starting your journey, this book will challenge, inspire, and equip you with the tools to lead with greater confidence and impact.

–Kory Dogs, Business & Executive Coach,
Owner, ActionCoach

HAVE WE MET?

HAVE WE MET?

DISCOVERING THE AUTHENTIC LEADER
YOU NEVER KNEW

JEREMY FYKE, PH.D.

ISBN: 979-8-9988506-1-5 (hardcover)
ISBN: 979-8-9988506-0-8 (paperback)
ISBN: 979-8-9988506-2-2 (ebook)

LCCN: 2025909245

For my partner and shotgun rider, Brooke,
who supports all my wild and crazy ideas.
I love you deeply and fiercely.

Table of Contents

Section IV
Openness & Action: The Keys for Authentic Leader Development

Section V
Sustaining Growth for a Lifetime

Appendices

Introduction

There once was a man who was convinced, he was dead. Month after month, he fought with his wife to try to convince her of this. After finally giving up trying to convince him otherwise, she had an idea--she'd take him to a doctor so the doctor could convince him that he was, in fact, not dead.

The plan was to administer a few simple tests that would prove to him he was not dead. The logic was simple enough—dead men won't have a heartbeat, blood pressure, or rising and falling breath, among other things. After a few minutes and a quick pulse check, the man exclaimed, "See, dead men do have a pulse!"

To be authentic is to be closely aligned to reality. Despite being quite a buzzword and mostly unquestioned quality, the reality in practice is that many leaders struggle to tap into the areas where they truly need work.

Part of the struggle with authenticity is that it has a "know it when you see it" quality. That's great when you see it and especially when you have it, but not so great when it comes to trying to actually develop it. The key to authentic leadership, however, lies in *how* the leader is developing, and that is something we can not only see but can control.

The key to authentic leadership is authentic *leader development*. It must be about the person, not the skills. It's about the person you are now and the person you're becoming. Too often, leaders focus on the tangible manifestation of who they are (leadership) without dealing with their underlying patterns, habits, and commitments (leader). For our purposes, we are going to define **authenticity in leadership simply as** *seeing yourself as a work in progress*.[1] More on this in the next chapter.

I want you to get a lot out of this book. Why wouldn't I, right? But seriously, I get so excited thinking about you reading this right now. I want to help you discover the leader you've never met before. Hence, the title of this book.

Credit for the inspiration for the title goes to my good friend Brandon Petty. Brandon is the founding, lead pastor of Generation Church just outside Nashville, Tennessee. Brandon is not only an impressive leader, people developer, and church planter. He's all those things, and he's among the very best at them of anyone I know. But Brandon's probably the most *intentional* person I know. He reflects, he plans, he sets aside time for things, he says no to things. This level of intentionality guides everything he does, and it influences a saying he and his church adopted many years ago: "There's a you you haven't met yet." By emphasizing the process of development–personal, spiritual–you can best see, and become, the person God created you to be.

So, there's the inspiration for the title of this book, applied to leader development: no matter who you are, where you are, how experienced you are, there's a leader you haven't met. The great theologian N.T. Wright, in his book *After You*

---

[1]   Barra, Herminia. *"The Authenticity Paradox," Emotional Intelligence: Authentic Leadership.* Harvard Business Review, 2018.

Believe writes, "The authenticity that really matters is living in accordance with the genuine human being God is calling you to become" (p. 108)[2]. Although a theological discussion like this is way beyond the scope of this book, I couldn't agree more with Wright's position. I believe God created us to live out an assignment here on earth. For our purposes in this book, that assignment looks like leadership in the form of service to others. The very best version of us–of you–is out there. She's out there. He's out there. More accurately, she's *in* there. That's right. **It's what's inside that counts**. It's the commitments you make to yourself. It's how intentional you are. It's your identity. It's your seriousness about your development. It's your mindsets. Crucially, it's how willing you are to practice, to do the hard work of development. This is the form of authentic leadership and authentic leader development I hope to help you with in this book.

I want to be clear about something important up front. And what I'm about to say is not merely semantics. I'm an academic by trade, so I can do semantics well, but I have no interest in doing that in this book. I wrote a Ph.D. dissertation at Purdue where I did plenty of that business!

This book is about authentic *leader* development. Not authentic leader*ship* or even authentic leadership *development*. I had a pastor friend who had a favorite line he would say when he was really convicted about something in the Bible. He'd say, "I know that I know that I know _____." Well, I know that I know that I know that for *you* to be the leader you're meant to be, and, practically speaking, to be most effective, you need to focus on you more than just what you *do*. Let me say it again–it's about *you*, not just what you

---

[2]   Wright, N.T. *After You Believe: Why Christian Character Matters.* HarperOne, 2012.

do. Yes, leadership and leading is what you do, but a leader is who you are. You must focus on who you are, who you're becoming. When you focus there first, then your habits, behaviors and all the things you do to execute and get results become more focused, more sustained.

We'll get into this more later, but for now, if you focus on leadership and leading and the skills you need to do that more effectively without focusing deeper, you'll just be the same you, but perhaps with more tools on your toolbelt. You'll try new stuff, and it might stick for a while, but chances are it won't sustain. I'm confident it won't serve you well in the long run because you'll end up reverting back to where you started. Deep change is what I'm after. And the best part—your leadership, leading, and behaviors will improve. We're just not starting there or emphasizing it. You with me?

With that in mind, let me be upfront about my goals. I have four, and they're why I'm so excited that you're reading this book.

After and while reading this book and working through the tools and practices, I pray you will—

1. Know yourself better.

2. Adopt a "work-in-progress" mentality for your life.

3. Work on yourself as much as you work on work.

4. Learn a bunch of things you can and will teach others.

First, I want you to get to know you, really well. As you read that, it might sound odd, maybe overly psychological, or even philosophical. But self-knowledge is critical and, as it turns out, could not get more practical when it comes to concrete skill development. The truth is, we don't really know ourselves all that well. I'll get into this more later, but briefly, people are largely unaware of how unaware of themselves they really are. But not only do I want you to get to know yourself better, to be clear, I want you to know yourself more accurately. You guessed it, more *authentically*. What makes you tick? Why do you keep trying some things, but those things don't stick? What are your tendencies, triggers, hang-ups, when it comes to how you lead others and lead yourself? These are some of the questions we'll explore in this book, but also ones I want to encourage you to ask throughout your life.

Second, **authenticity isn't a state or a destination; it's a process**. It's a lifelong process. As I mentioned above, I define authenticity as seeing yourself as a work in progress. Therefore, my goal is for you to adopt this mindset of seeing yourself as a work in progress and take that with you into the people, situations, and companies you are blessed to lead. When you adopt a work-in-progress mentality, you do two things.

First, you're intentional about working on yourself at all times and in all situations. For example, if you're working on your leadership presence—something I work on often—you begin to identify triggers that throw you off at work and at home. You might be trying to have a moment with your daughter while she's practicing her reading on the couch, but you keep getting distracted by your notifications on your phone, or perhaps more insidious, the thoughts of your to-do list in your mind. Are you working parents tracking with me here?! When one of your account executives comes to you needing support, you half-listen because the meeting you just had with another account executive is on your mind. We've all been there. The goal is to notice your tendencies (see goal number one) and then start to use those as data for further development.

But secondly, when you adopt a work-in-progress mentality, you give yourself grace. I realize I just said you work on yourself all the time, but I'm not contradicting myself here. It's a both-and proposition. You view situations from the standpoint of what they can teach you and, at the same time, you aren't perfect, hence, work in progress. When you mess up, you learn from it, reflect, make some future commitments to yourself and others, and move on.

My third goal for you, and hopefully you're seeing how these things build on each other, is that you are as focused on you and your development as you are on the work you get paid to do. You work on yourself as much as you work on your work. We'll get into this in a later chapter, but as leaders, we tend to focus on getting stuff done—your tasks, responsibilities, projects, reports, KPIs, right? We need to get those done, so please don't stop. But, while you're leading all of those things—in other words, executing—it's imperative that you lead yourself well. What does that look like? You know when people ask you how you've been, and you say "busy"? Chances are, you're thinking of all you've been doing and stuff you've been getting done. Well, working on yourself needs to be part of that "busy." In this book I'll give you a bunch of tools, tips, and methods you can use to reflect, plan, and work on yourself. Some tools are more long-term in nature, ones you need to use over multiple instances. Other tools are ones you can use in the moment, in more discrete instances to gain insight into your communication and leadership habits in a single shot.

I have one final goal for you, and this is where your investment, in the time you spend reading this and putting the tools into practice, has a compounding effect. I want you to learn a lot that you can and will teach to others. In fact, the final chapter in the book shows you some concrete ways to teach what you learn and help grow others. Leadership, leading, and communication are all highly teachable. Anytime you learn something new, and, crucially, you start putting it into practice, the value of it compounds when you can teach it to someone else. Oftentimes that teaching looks like sitting down and sharing what you learn. I love hearing stories from former clients about how they took a tool such as Mental Replay (see Chapter 6) and used it with their teams. Explicit teaching and trying out new things are powerful.

Another, and I would argue, more potent and sustainable form of teaching, is through modeling. When your people see you communicating differently, reflecting more, and being more intentional, they will want to respond in kind. I believe they will, and plenty of science backs that up. When you demonstrate to them how to reflect and ask questions, and you start asking them to hold you accountable, it will impact the culture. It's difficult for it not to. You've probably heard the saying that culture is top-down but driven bottom-up, in other words, it is owned by leaders *and* employees[3]. So it is with leader development. When your people see you developing and working on yourself, they want to get in on it too.

Quick story. Recently I had a leader stop me in the hallway after a workshop. He told me about how one of his direct reports recently called him out on something. It really challenged him, in the best of ways. His direct report had been dealing with a difficult customer for about the last month. She felt like she was making progress, but this leader was getting frustrated, so he started stepping in, at one point,

---

[3] *Shaping Company Culture from the Top Down and Bottom Up.* Hunt Scanlon Media, 2023

literally calling the customer himself to try to resolve the situation. In a candid conversation, his direct report told him, "I know you were trying to help, but when you step in like that it makes me feel like you don't trust me." He said it was a splash of cold water to the face. After a bit more conversation, I learned that he had recently started a practice of check-ins and direct feedback with his direct reports. He challenged them, they challenged him. See, it was powerful what the direct report was doing, but all she was doing was modeling what she had seen. Simple, but profound.

So, there you have it. My cards are on the table. You know what I hope and pray for you as you read the pages that follow. I can't wait to hear stories like the one above that you share with me in the coming months and years. But **the key is your commitment and seriousness about putting these tools to work**. If you're ready to put in the work, here's what you can expect in the pages that follow.

Preview

This book unfolds in five sections. Section one offers context for my story, my journey toward authentic development, and the various places, spaces, and opportunities we all have for developing into the authentic leader we're meant to be. We'll also explore tendencies—good and bad—we all have when we work on ourselves. As it turns out, if we're not careful, these tendencies are our enemies toward sustained change and growth. Section one ends with a discussion of three levels of leadership, a perspective that helps place our developmental goals in their proper context.

Section two explores part one of a two-part leader development framework: openness. We'll look at four crucial practices to help you be open to development and growth: vulnerability, authenticity, reflection, and projection.

Section three explores part two of a two-part leader development framework: action. In addition to being open to development, you must put what you learn into practice in meaningful ways. To get there, you'll learn techniques for practicing small, measuring your progress, and practicing accountability.

Section four brings sections two and three together to present a 2x2 Model of Authentic Leader Development based on the two factors previously noted: openness and action. I show how the combination of these two factors produces four "profiles" of leader development—some productive, some unproductive. My goal here is for you to be able to see yourself and others through this framework. This will help you help yourself and others toward sustained growth and development.

Finally, in section five, I'll show how to consolidate and sustain gains for a lifetime. You'll learn techniques for applying what you learn on the job and in collaboration with others. The final chapter shows you how to take what you learn and model it for others as you work to serve them and help with *their* growth, arguably the pinnacle of leader development.

Before we jump into content, let me say a few more things about the tone of the book and how you can maximize your investment in it. As I alluded to earlier, this is meant to be a practical book, a how-to guide for developing authentically. Yes, the techniques are backed by research, which you will see in the references as you go, but my main goal in the pages that follow is to offer you a bevy of tools, techniques, and resources you can put into practice immediately. In the appendix you'll find a complete list of the tools and frameworks suggested in the book, along with references and further readings, when applicable. You are busy and I want you to get a lot out of your investment, including and especially, your time in reading this book! Finally, in preparation for writing, I interviewed 20 leaders across various industries and levels of leadership to hear their stories and get their take on authentic leader development. At the end of the book, in Appendix B, you'll find some key takeaways and ideas from those conversations, organized as "Leader Lessons" on multiple topics of interest. My hope is that those are insightful and helpful as you work on your personal leader development.

With that in mind, you'll get plenty of uses out of this book if you are in any of the following groups. One caveat that applies to many of these: you don't have to be in a formal leadership role to benefit from this book. John Maxwell, arguably the world's foremost leadership expert, is known for saying, "leadership isn't about titles, positions, or flowcharts; it's about one life influencing another." That's it. Leadership is about influence, as well as activity and relationships. You might be reading this as an individual contributor in an organization and not a formal people leader by title. Take the practices and use them anyway. Everything you read in here will serve you well now and when you get into a formal leadership seat someday, if you choose to do so.

Beyond that, here's how to get the most out of this book for:

Students

As a college educator, there's nothing more rewarding that I get to do than help you develop! I don't just see my role as teaching you interesting stuff; I'm helping you develop lifelong leadership skills. Regardless of your age or level in school, you will find this book useful. Perhaps you've had some leadership roles already in student organizations, at work, or at church. You might find some of the examples hard to relate to if you don't have a lot of formal work experience. That's ok; take notes anyway and learn from the examples you read about. Many of the practices you read about can be put into action immediately by anyone at any level. It's never too early to begin thinking about and working on the leader you are created to be. Lastly, the perspectives in this book might just give you some ideas of the type of work you want to do and more importantly the type of culture you want to do it in. You should seek employment somewhere that values your growth and development. I hope what you read here raises your standards for where you want to spend so much of life: work!

Team Members/Employees

If you're not in a formal leadership role, it's never too early to be intentionally cultivating the leadership brand you want. If you're not intentional about it, it might just be built in a way you don't want. Take charge of yourself and your leadership identity and brand by putting what you read into practice. I also encourage you to take the examples you read about and practices I suggest here and use them as conversation points with your leaders. Talk to them about their practices, their leadership, and their opportunities, challenges, and best practices. As a bonus: identify a leader you can read this with and then work through the techniques together. Additionally, I recommend you get a group of your peers and read this together. Share goals, wins, and challenges. Finally, if you feel that you don't have sufficient leader development opportunities in your organization, you have a lot of ideas in here that you can push for.

People Leaders

Leader, you are in a seat of great influence. If you're reading this book, you probably know that; you feel it. You might have picked this book up because you're tired. Or maybe you're bored. Maybe you've been involved in a lot of leadership development initiatives, projects, and events over the years. Perhaps a lot of things have worked and perhaps a lot of things didn't. You might be reading this because you can't get enough of leadership development and are excited about what I have to offer. Regardless of where you are, I'm glad you're reading. My encouragement to you is simple: begin with an open mind and commit to trying new things out. As you'll read about, I'll encourage you to "practice small" by emphasizing incremental progress based on authentic reflection. As you try stuff out, don't go it alone. I encourage you to read this book with at least one other person. Even better, get a group of four or five of your colleagues together to read it and work through the exercises together. The benefit is compounded when you collaborate and share wins and challenges. Every tool in here can be shared, discussed, and scaled up to a larger group for discussion and application.

L&D Practitioners

If you are a learning and development or human resources professional, a people development officer, or any similar position, I encourage you to scale up your reading and application of this book. Have your trainers, coaches, and facilitators read it and work through the tools and practices together. As you do, aim for a "cascading" effect where the practices can then be applied throughout teams in the organization for a wider impact. Finally, be sure you are taking care of yourself as you read this book. You are likely in a leadership role yourself, and you need to continue to sharpen your saw as well. My experience is that it's all too easy for L&D practitioners, particularly in higher roles, to neglect their own growth.

SECTION I

We're in This Together

This first section begins on a personal note, as I take you into my story and paint a picture for what authentic leader development looks like in my life. We'll also look at the various contexts in which we can develop and otherwise work on ourselves. As it turns out, the contexts are vast and wide, so the more we know what those are on the front end, the better off we are so we can spot opportunities and be intentional. I'll also talk about several things that stand in our way when we try to develop—including and especially ourselves. We'll end Section I with a look at three levels of leadership, which provide a crucial perspective for helping us develop ourselves as we work to serve others and execute. Let's get started!

1

My Story, Our Contexts

Nice to Meet You!

This is a book about authenticity, so I feel it's important for me to take you into my story for a bit so we can get to know each other. Who I am influences how I lead and how I develop. It's what people see when I'm doing what God put me on this earth to do.

I alluded to this earlier, but I'm an academic by trade. Basically, that means that in my full-time work I get to teach college students. I say "get to" because it's such a huge blessing and I consider it an honor. Does it always feel that way when I'm in the middle of a semester and writing my 100th comment in a week about writing using active voice or addressing me as "hey" in an email? Not always. But for the most part, it's the biggest blessing and highest calling for me that I can imagine. I just love what I do.

What I love about it is that beyond teaching students I see my role as a people developer. I experience people in their late teens and early twenties, which you might know are some important years. We're coming into who we are, we're weird and awkward, we're influenced by just about everything around us, and we're at the perfect point in life to be learning some critical development habits. Beyond just the topics I teach, I want to play a role in helping students form those habits. Habits such as open-mindedness and creativity, critical thinking, and self-awareness.

Outside of the college classroom, I get to develop leaders. Early on in my graduate work I knew this is what I wanted to be when I grew up. I was in a graduate-level Corporate Training and Development course taught by Dr. Steve Beebe, someone who ended up being a mentor and friend. He was talking about the business of training and development, and I specifically remember him telling us what he charged for a full-day workshop. At that point, I said to myself, that's what I want to do! The vision of the practitioner-academic was born in my head.

I refer to myself as a "pracademic." Yes, I have a Ph.D., and I can talk academic talk and write in academic speak. I did my Ph.D. at Purdue, where I studied Organizational Communication with a minor in Human Behavior and Human Resources. Basically, things like effective communication, leadership, organizational culture, and developmental psychology get me really excited.

But early on in my career I knew I wasn't going to be content only teaching in a college classroom. I don't say that to throw shade (college students keep me up on my cool lingo) on college professors that "just" teach. It's a good life, a good living, with plenty of purpose, income, and stress for a full-time career. But for me, I couldn't see how I could study communication and leaders in the workplace and not spend some time in, well, workplaces. Also, I just love business, watching businesses, and learning from them. I've often had a creative streak in me when it came to business, so in late 2020 I founded a hot sauce company, Two Heads Hot Sauce, a business I ran with a buddy of mine for nearly four years and sold in 2024. I learned more in that four years about business and leadership than I could have ever imagine. It made me appreciate leadership, leaders, and leader development even more.

What I've been consumed with over my career is the *process* **of development**—how students develop, how leaders develop. For example, in the speech classroom, I talk about how to deliver an effective speech, but the process of preparing for one and the habits that come with that is where the magic happens. In a training seminar or keynote with 200 leaders, yes, we talk about Executive Presence, but the habits you form and practice in sync with the specific skills are where I love to spend a lot of time.

In the early 2010s, I brought my academic background and professional aspirations together to launch my training business, Jeremy Fyke Leader Development (now called Authentic Leader Development). My passion for the process of development and conviction about the leader being the most important factor in development—rather than just the skills—led me to intentionally use the word *Leader* in the name of my business, rather than calling it Jeremy Fyke Leadership Development. This is not semantics, so take a second to let that sink in. **It's about who you're becoming and developing into much more than what you're learning— it's** *who* **before** *do*. It's a both-and proposition, but the order makes a big difference. In other words, emphasize *who* you are becoming first and often, and the rest will fall into place.

In the introduction I defined authenticity as seeing your-self as a work in progress. This definition is a mantra that I live by, as my close friends, colleagues, and family members will attest. I'm constantly working on myself, so much so that giving myself grace to mess up and just be human is a strug-gle at times. I love developing people, including myself. Rest assured, there's nothing in this book that I don't use person-ally. As I tell all my training clients, "I walked in here today with a limp, not a swagger." We're in this together.

I share these portions of my background because they directly influence how I approach leader development, and how I want to encourage you throughout this book. Yes, skills are valuable, but process is where the magic happens. Fortunately for all of us, there are plenty of places and spaces where we can practice. We turn there next.

Our Contexts: Where we Develop

At the outset it's important to say a few words about *where* leader development might take place. What comes to mind when you think of leader/ship development? Is it formal training sessions you've attended? Perhaps execu-tive coaching? Or is it less formal such as when you take it upon yourself to read a self-help book on leadership or take courses on LinkedIn Learning to sharpen your skills? These are all "contexts" for leader development; that is, places/methods where leader development happens. I'll talk in a little bit about best practices, what's most effective, etc., but suffice it to say that **the important thing isn't so much where and how development takes place but that it does, in fact, take place.** In other words, commit to lifelong learning and growing and don't worry too much about how formal or informal it is.

Throughout the book I'll reference a range of leader development contexts—formal and informal—so in this section let's get clear on some of those contexts. In laying out these contexts on the front end, I want to help you get a picture of what the possibilities might look like, but also encourage you to do some reflecting and planning, based on the rhythms and seasons of your life. You can look around your life, the culture of where you work, and the resources available (or not) to you and be better able to get to work applying what you read here. What I present here is by no stretch an exhaustive list, but it'll give a snapshot of some of the most common contexts.

First and perhaps most obviously, there is formal leader development via training. Training can then take various shapes including seminars led by an internal or external facilitator. Most of my leader development work with businesses takes this form—companies hire me to come in and facilitate a training workshop. Formal training can be one-off and topic-based, such as when a facilitator speaks to a group of leaders on a topic either based on company competencies, operating priorities, or values. Trainings can be a mixed cohort (i.e., individuals from across functions) or audience specific based on current needs. For example, I led two trainings recently for a group of licensing professionals in the music industry on the topic of critical thinking, problem-solving, and decision making. The music industry has undergone countless disruptions over the past decade, so training focused on thinking in different and creative ways was necessary.

Beyond one-off, topic-based trainings, leader development can occur in multi-session formats such as leadership academies. Yes, it is true that the most important factor in leader development is that it's happening in some fashion.

But the academy format is arguably the most effective way to drive leader development. My personal experience and emerging neuroscience research support this conclusion. Typically, a group of leaders from across functions comes together as a cohort, normally based on nominations from senior leadership. This cohort then goes through a curriculum designed either by the company or an external agent together over a period of time. For example, for several years I led numerous cohorts through a 20-week leadership academy. Each time, I had the privilege of leading 10-15 leaders, most new to a formal leadership role, through a variety of topics (e.g., conflict management, public speaking, managing change, professional presence). The leaders met with me bi-weekly and then in the off weeks from our session they met with a coach for group coaching and practice. In between sessions the leaders practiced what they learned and talked about their practice with their colleagues. (This in-between session work is one of the most effective but underutilized practices in leader development. But more on that later.) If your company has academy offerings like this available, run to them as fast as you can. If not, run to create or push for them as fast as you can! They take up a lot of your time and are a big cost investment, but it's worth it.

Another formal training method that I'm blessed to do quite a bit of is executive coaching. Although coaching is typically less formal than training, it normally begins with goals and outcomes in mind and is led by some coaching methods or frameworks known to the coach. For example, I worked with a C-level leader at a large multinational corporation recently who was looking to improve on his presence and presentation skills. We arrived at these goal areas in consultation with his senior leader. Coaching leverages open-ended questions to allow leaders to arrive at their own conclusions and generate solutions to common leadership challenges. Whereas trainers prepare content and teach tools and methods to trainees, coaches use questions to allow coachees to arrive at the help they need. There might be a "key" out there to figuring out a leader's challenges, but it's the coachee's responsibility to find that key. The coach facilitates that process.[4]

But leader development doesn't have to be as formal as training seminars or academies. When you take the initiative to read and learn on your own, you are investing in your leader development. You're "sharpening the saw," in Covey's 7 Habits language. We'll get into this more as the book unfolds, but the important thing is what you're doing while you're developing in terms of questions you're asking yourself, how intentional you are, what your reflection looks like, and so on. For instance, you can complete a "Leader Gap Analysis" (see Chapter 7) monthly, irrespective of any formal development methods, or in conjunction with your 4-month leadership academy you and your peers are engaged in. Likewise, a self-accountability practice like journaling is a powerful tool for development, whether at the beginning of a coaching partnership or as a standalone method while you're working through a good self-help book.

To reiterate, I presented these different contexts for you to consider for several reasons. First, perhaps you've not undertaken many formal training opportunities available to you, and this will give you an idea of things you can seek out. Or maybe your company has tended to favor one-off, topic-based trainings, something common in this space, and this overview gives you some fresh ideas for expanding your

---

[4]   Van Nieuwerburgh, C. *An Introduction to Coaching Skills* (2nd Ed.). Sage, 2017.

offerings. Another goal I have in presenting this overview though is to, in some ways, demystify leader development. We tend to overthink it and make it more than it has to be. No doubt, formal leader development paired with coaching synced up with your performance management system at your work is necessary and powerful for your growth. But what about outside of those formal methods? Chances are that the formal methods comprise a small portion of your time learning and developing anyway. Many of the tools and methods you'll find in this book are to help you in the 90% of learning that takes place outside a formal setting.[5] My principal goal here is to help you build a tool kit for intentional development for your lifetime.

Personalize it

I am reading this book because

My most recent//current leadership development experience is

My least impactful leadership development experiences have been

My most impactful leadership development experiences have been

When I have grown the most in my leadership development, it has been because

2

Opposition: The Forces that Work Against Progress

Throughout my 20+ year career of full-time teaching, training, and coaching leaders, I've noticed that people are their own worst enemy when it comes to growth and development. Yes, time constraints and other "external" factors weigh on us all, but often, we get in our own way—a lot. This chapter highlights a few obstacles that impede our progress toward personal and professional leader development. Most importantly, my call to action for you as you read this is to do a bit of self-assessment. Ask yourself, where have you seen these things play out for you and get in your way? How can you relate to the behaviors and tendencies described below? I'll include some additional prompts as relevant for each of the observations that follow.

There are many things we could discuss here, but I most often notice three tendencies in people, their development, and what they're looking for:

1. People are hungry to learn, hungry for tools (hacks).

2. People don't reflect nearly as much as they should. And because of that...

3. People miss out on opportunities for sustained, authentic development.

The Hunger for Hacks

"15 Tips for Effective Communication."

"The 7 Cs of Effective Communication for Leaders."

"8 Essential Leadership Communication Skills."

"The 6 Skills the Best Leaders Have."

A quick browse or Google search for effective leadership communication reveals virtually limitless advice. Most of this advice is in the form of actions, tips, and tricks. It makes sense given the attention economy we live in. After all, a best practice for search engine optimization (SEO) is to write your articles in such a way as to deliver 3 of these, 6 of that. There is so much information but only so much attention to go around.

To be clear, there isn't anything necessarily wrong with tips and advice. Something is better than nothing. As an educator, I see an appetite for learning, and that makes me excited. I see the hunger for learning first-hand, whether I'm leading workshops or coaching people one-on-one. Depending on the occasion, tips have their place. When I train a group of 100 people at a large corporation, they will likely feel like it wasn't worth their time if they don't leave with a few concrete, quick things they can take with them. Learning a new skill often starts with advice on how to do something differently and hopefully better.

But basing your leader development solely on tips and advice is simply incomplete at best and, I argue, misguided at worst. What I tell every audience, no matter the size, no matter their reason for being there, is that **if they don't take what they learn and reflect on it in relation to who they are, their story, their journey, and where they want to go, it will amount to nothing more than a hack, a new thing to try out.** We'll explore how to reflect on who you are, your story, etc. a little later, but for now, let's learn to identify the danger in relying on hacks.

In computer lingo, hacks are what actors (oftentimes bad) use to bypass traditional means of accessing information or completing tasks. In less formal terms, a hack is "a clever tip or technique for doing or improving something."[6] Therefore, "life hacks" are things—shortcuts—we do to make life easier. Again, picking up a hack or two here and there (e.g., a tip to help you manage your time) isn't necessarily bad. But my contention, with the support of loads of emerging neuroscience research, is that **there are some things in life where there are no shortcuts. Sustained development is one of those things.** What research shows us is that things we learn, for example in workshops or other formal settings, most of the time end up being things we try out as new actions that simply don't stick long term. Ultimately, they don't lead to

---

[6]   "Hack." Merriam-Webster.

new habits, new ways of doing things.[7] To push it further, they don't stick because they don't lead to new ways of *being*. True development isn't about doing things differently, it's about being a different person, a different leader.

We'll discuss ways of being who you want to be and how to develop who you want to be a little later, but for now, reflect and do an assessment on the following:

- What "hacks" or shortcuts were presented to you during the last training or development session you attended?

- How did you take what you learned and put it into practice?

- What difference did those tips make in your leadership?

- How sustained were the changes/the differences?

Our Reflection Defection

The pace of life is a big enemy to one of the most critical elements of sustained development: our ability to slow down and reflect. "I don't have time to reflect, I'm too busy acting." I hear a version of this quite often from people I train and coach. I'll spend quite a bit of time on reflection in Chapter 4, but I wanted you to read it here on the front end of the book so you can assess where you are in relation to reflecting. If you're honest (another chapter itself!) how often do you

---

[7]   Fast Company. "Leadership Development is Broken: Here's How to Fix It." 2024.

reflect? I mean sit down to reflect, not just think to yourself "well, that went well today" after you leave the meeting.

My experience is that people do not practice this skill well, if at all. I call it a skill because I want to emphasize that it should be something you are intentional about practicing, just like you would intentionally incorporate other things into your leadership repertoire (e.g., active listening, effective eye contact). In our modern-day busy lives, leaders don't spend much time slowing down long enough to think and examine their days as communicators, as leaders.

- What does reflection look like for you?

- How do you practice self-awareness?

- When was the last time you sat down to reflect?

- When you do reflect, what are the results?

- What do you do with the "information" you get from reflection?

So, by and large, people don't reflect nearly as often as they should. I bet if you're honest, this is true for you. I know it is for me! This fact leads to the third and final observation, which is the most unfortunate and counterproductive of all.

You're Missing Out

When we commit to using hacks rather than changing our ways of being *and* we don't plan times to intentionally reflect, we miss out on so many opportunities for true, sustained development. The interesting and counterintuitive reality too is that slowing down and reflecting on deep changes will set us up to be better in the future where we don't need hacks in the first place. Yes, slow down to eventually speed up. It's not that you won't continue to learn new things and try new techniques out; it's just that those tips and techniques will fall in line with who you are and who you are becoming.

If this seems abstract, let's explore a quick example to illustrate. Let's say you're wanting to improve your leadership presence. Even more specifically, you're wanting to be a better listener by learning to compartmentalize and block out distractions. Chances are being a leader affords you countless opportunities to practice any new technique you might learn (e.g., "active listening"). Rather than simply practicing a new technique like active listening, deep, authentic development would ask you to identify the larger "why" behind being a better listener in the first place. You want to be seen as fully available to your team so you can maximize your influence and empower them to be their best. Once you do that, then you can use that to reflect often about how you "show up" to others. When Joe, your project manager, left the meeting, how did you show up for him? Were you hurried, scattered, and unfocused? Or were you measured, calm, and focused on him and his concerns, his agenda? Reflecting on questions like these then will give you a compass point to keep you heading in the right direction. And, importantly, the preceding is an example of how to place your development in a larger context, so that when you learn a tip or technique, you then begin to see each new or routine communication as an opportunity to be the leader you want to be.

With those observations as a backdrop, let's explore two forces that oppose our sustained growth and development. We're our own worst enemy when it comes to change and growth, even though we might come by these honestly and out of limited time and bandwidth. I bet you've seen these in yourself. I see them standing in my way all the time. Do an honest appraisal and see how they apply to you. As leaders, we tend to overestimate our strengths. Additionally, as we'll see in a bit, we resist change in ourselves nearly as much (or perhaps more) as we do external change.

I'm Good At...

Excellence in business and leadership is predicated on, well, being excellent at whatever it is you are tasked with doing. Whether it's casting vision, being the architect of a new strategic plan, increasing sales, reducing customer complaints in your call center, whatever it is. Job descriptions call for competency and people get promoted and rewarded for being great. Don't get me wrong: greatness is a good thing! I'm not calling for substandard work or the lowering of standards. A high functioning, free-market, capitalist society only works when people perform at their best. The danger comes in when people overestimate their strengths to the point where they stop learning, stop seeing areas for improvement.

One way this creeps in is how our society, particularly in business, values knowing over questioning. Reports show that kids ask some 40,000 questions by the age of five.[8] Side note: if you've ever traveled on a road trip with a kid or two in the backseat, you might be feeling, like me, that 40k is a low-ball estimate. Whatever the number, the reality is that as we age, and as we move up the ranks in our careers especially, we pride ourselves on knowledge and competency. After all, isn't business acumen—what you know and can do—highly prized in the workplace?

---

[8] Berger, Warren. *A More Beautiful Question: The Power of Inquiry to Spark Breakthrough Ideas.* Bloomsburg USA, 2012.

Business acumen should be prized. We want people who know their stuff. But here's the rub: This preference for knowing not only applies in decision-making and execution, but also in our own development in two ways. First, if and when we take this preference for knowing into our own work on ourselves, **we tend to overestimate our own strengths**. We don't question our own abilities, especially the more experience we gather. This just creates blind spots that can take months or years to spot, let alone start to correct.

I recently coached a leader who had many years of experience as a corporate executive. He transitioned into a new role about a year before I began coaching him. In his new role, his boss, the CEO, told him she needed him to take on a more active role with the team and to begin taking more "ownership" over different areas of the organization. In brief, if there were areas he didn't feel were best in line with his competency or interest, he would check out. The CEO perceived a lack of trust between him and the team because he didn't seem to stay engaged or plugged in with the teams he was leading. He didn't see it as a lack of trust at all and frankly didn't perceive any issues whatsoever. His years of experience had created natural blind spots. It was a classic case of "nothing to see here." He thought he was doing a great job because of what he was good at; others saw it differently. Blind spots like these get in our way of growth and place lids over our leadership that are virtually impossible to break through without reflection.

Another way this "knowing over questioning" creeps in is when we try to figure things out on our own. We don't ask for help, and we don't bring others into our growth journey. In a brief but powerful testament to this fact, *Harvard Business Review* writes, "Despite our common cultural notion of 'self' improvement, the most successful efforts to self-improve have other people at their core."[9] We don't like to admit when we need help, so we make development a solo enterprise. In Chapter 8 I'll share some best practices for bringing others into your development journey as accountability partners. For now, let me encourage you: when it comes to your development, don't go at it alone. You don't have all the answers and more often than not, people see you better than you see you, especially when it comes to things that are external such as communication. You may think you're a good listener, but the people that you lead know how you really show up to them. You don't have to wonder what they think—just ask! And the more you ask and the more they share, you can begin to break down your resistance to that feedback, another force that opposes our efforts to develop.

I Might Need to Change, but I Doubt It (or, I just don't want to)

Here's a simple truth: resistance to change applies to ourselves as much as "external" things. A short peek into developmental psychology research shows that we build up a natural immunity to change, much like the body builds up an immunity to infection. Through routines and habits, we learn to avoid things that cause us discomfort, in turn making it harder to change. When doctors tell seriously at-risk heart patients that they must make fundamental changes to their lives—e.g., diet, exercise, stop smoking—or they will die, only one in seven actually do it. One in seven.[10] When

---

[9]   *Rely on Others to Improve Yourself.* Harvard Business Review, 2017.
[10]   Kegan, Robert & Lahey, Lisa. *Immunity to Change.* Harvard Business Review Press, 2009.

the consequences are literally life or death, we don't have a good track record of success when it comes to change.

This truth applies to our ability or lack thereof to change things about ourselves. We learn to do things a certain way, to react and show up to people a certain way, and that gets comfortable. If someone presents information that runs contrary to how we do things, we have one major tendency. We are more likely to change the information rather than our behavior. It's a fact about most feedback we receive. We qualify the information ("well, at least I wasn't a 5/10 on listening from all my employees") or rationalize it ("I know I didn't do well last month, but I was really swamped"). Worse yet, we change it altogether ("Kendra sees it as a lack of trust, but she's just wrong about that"). I see this play out all the time when I coach and train leaders.

I bring this one in at the end because it's the most prevalent and the most damaging to our ability to grow and develop as leaders and as humans. When we question the information or change the feedback, we miss out. If someone brings us information that runs contrary to how we see ourselves, at the very least, we must engage with that information and do some internal "fact checking." More on this later... For now, as I end this chapter, I want you to do a bit of reflecting.

- Where have you seen these tendencies show up in your life?

- How often do you ask questions about yourself and your abilities?

- How honest are you about your own strengths and weaknesses?

- When it comes to development, do you tend to go at it alone? Why?

- What are the benefits and drawbacks to having an accountability partner in your leadership development?

- If you've never had an accountability partner for your leadership development, why not?

- The last time someone gave you feedback on your leadership, how did you respond?

- Whether you accepted it or not, what did you do with that feedback?

Personalize It

Where do you find the "hunger for hacks" impacting you and your life?

How often do you reflect? If not much at all, why not? What gets in the way of your reflection?

Identify two habits you could start today to help you reflect more often:

1. _____

2. _____

Identify a recent time when you resisted change, including a need for personal and/or leadership development change.

3

Who Before Do

There's more to you than what you do. Let that sink in for a minute. More specifically, there's more to you as a leader and to your leadership than your tasks, projects, and accomplishments. Yes, you must execute and get results. And you must think about and work on yourself and your leadership. It's a both/and proposition. And that's the hard part.

To help you think through and prioritize the both/and-ness of it, it's critical to set a foundation early on in this book on three levels of leadership: Leading Self, Leading Others, Leading Initiatives. As you can probably gather from a glance at the three levels, there are things we are expected to do and there are people we lead. But the part we forget or neglect is the person at the center of it—us. Here's the main takeaway: **it's extremely difficult—if not impossible—to lead others well and get things done effectively in the long**

term if you're not leading yourself well. In this chapter we explore these three levels together. For each, I'll offer some key activities that are most likely present to you to help illustrate the different levels. My task for you is to follow along by noting things that fit in these different levels. Importantly, however, I challenge you to be honest about areas of strength and development for you.

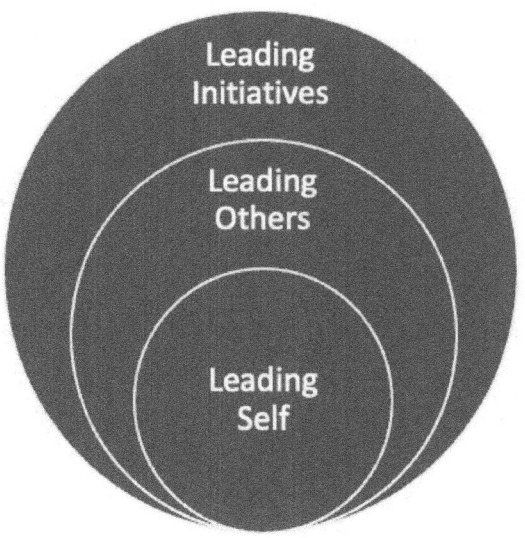

For many of us, level three—leading initiatives—is a sweet spot, a comfort zone. This is where you get to (hopefully) work on projects and accomplish tasks that are in your wheelhouse. Chances are, these things are in your job description. You also do many things at this level that are not on your job description, right? What "initiatives" means and includes varies greatly. Depending on your position in the organization, your scope of responsibility might be narrow or wide. Level three for you might include big, strategic projects or smaller, more tactical things. You might oversee the entire Employee Experience unit, or you might draft job descriptions to help recruit new talent. You might oversee the Organization Development unit, or you might design PowerPoints for internal leadership training offerings. Another way to think about level three is leading *impact* or *outcomes*—the results you get, or are expected to get, from your efforts. If you own your own business, as I do, level three looks and sounds more like "leading the business." At this level, you're developing and casting vision, doing short, medium, and long-term strategic planning, and trying to grow the business.

Previously, I said this might be a comfort zone because if we're being honest, there's indeed comfort in getting to just focus on getting stuff done. "Nothing motivates like progress," as the saying goes. After all, we know that mastery—the desire to get better at things—is a key internal motivator that drives people.[11] It's a beautiful thing to have stuff to do, things to work on, projects to tackle. If you're a to-do list, checklist type of person, this stuff makes your heart sing. But there's more to it than that.

Level two—leading others—is where the real stuff of leadership comes into play. This level is about, wait for it, leading other people. It's about building relationships, getting things done (level one) through other people, and crucially, empowering them to get things done. Again, depending on your scope of responsibility, you might have a few "others" to lead or a large department. I trained a leader recently who led a team in an academic unit at a college with 55 faculty under him. His leadership and what he simply has the bandwidth

---

[11]   Pink, Daniel. *Drive: The Surprising Truth about What Motivates Us.* Penguin, 2009.

to do looks different than someone with three direct reports. Same ideas and goals perhaps, but different execution, assuming everyone has the same number of hours in the day.

Beyond the direct connection between other people and the tasks they/you are responsible for, at this level you also have coaching, mentoring, serving, and supporting your people. Again, this is the true stuff of leadership. Leadership is about service. I read something years ago that rocked my world. The English word "leadership" contains the ancient root *leith*, which meant "go forth and die." How's that for servant-minded, sacrificial leadership? Most early conceptions of leadership had military applications, so that viewpoint makes sense. Today, we exist in relatively safe environments, especially in the west, so unless you are in the military or are former military, the original intent of the term might not land as squarely. Still, the translation points to the seriousness of being a leader. It's about other people, and it's sweaty, stressful, hard, and sometimes downright inconvenient. Remember, getting stuff done is the comfort zone!

In level two, being able to move from just a manager of things and projects to leader-as-coach is critical. Here, skills such as active listening, being a compelling communicator, and leveraging the strengths of those around you are vital. These are the people-based, "soft" skills that come in handy with other people. I can't begin to tell you how many leaders I've trained and coached over the years who are second-to-none at their roles, tasks, and responsibility, but just can't connect with people. Level two is where they struggle.

I invite you here to do a quick assessment of your skills at this level. What are your strengths and what are your areas for improvement? I'll go first. I can work quickly and get stuff done fast (level one). Where I've struggled as a leader is waiting for others and then providing them the help and coaching they need to be successful. I need to work on meeting people where they are, knowing they're not likely as far along as I am or would like them to be. As I begin to reflect on my skills at this level, I'm able to explore the next level of leadership.

Level one leadership—leading self—is what makes the magic of leadership possible, at least in the long term. Recall what I said at the start—it will be difficult, if not impossible to lead others well and be successful at your job, *in the long term*, if you don't lead yourself well. What comes to mind when you read leading self? No need to overcomplicate it, so let's just define it as *working on yourself.* Simple. Not easy, but simple. I submit to you that you can get stuff done and connect with people for a period of time, but you will burn out, struggle to adapt, and lose your effectiveness as a leader if you are not working on yourself.

When you work on yourself, you are intentional about your development. More on that shortly. You spot growth areas constantly. You are receptive to feedback. When someone shares feedback, you listen with an open mind. If there are parts to the feedback that contradict what others have said or that contradict your self-concept, you don't reject the feedback; you engage it. That is, you go to the person who shared it and discuss it.

One of the funny things about feedback that makes it hard and frankly ineffective most of the time, is due to our human tendencies. Our egos work hard to try to protect us. We have a tiny part of our brain called the amygdala that serves as the emotion center of our brains. It's the part that gets activated when something scares us. If you're jogging and you hear something rustle in the bushes, you jump and get out of the way. It's helpful when it protects us. Unfortunately, that same tiny, emotion-first part of our brain is also what kicks in when we get feedback, particularly negative information. That amygdala receives the information and initiates the fight or flight response. The bottom line: **when we get feedback, it's hardwired in us to change the information we get rather than our behavior to protect ourselves**. The "threats" to ourselves are as potent as perceived physical threats.[12] Leaders who lead themselves well don't do that. They might not like the feedback or relate to it right away—it might even sting a little—but they listen to it and consider its validity. They tell that emotion-first part of their brain to hush so they can process it logically and with intentionality.

Again, leading yourself well is about working on yourself. Knowing what to work on and how, and then being intentional about it. We'll talk a lot in this book about authenticity—it's what the book is about, after all! But I submit to you that **authenticity's core prerequisite is intentionality**.

You will read the word "intentional" or "intentionality" often in this book. Beyond that, you may have noticed it is quite a buzz word in many circles from self-help to business. That's for good reason. When it comes to development, especially sustained development, you can make the argument that there's hardly a more important "X-factor." It tends to have a compounding effect. Try something and be intentional about it. Work on yourself in area _____ and do so intentionally. When we are intentional about things, good things happen. By contrast, when we're unintentional, our efforts are shallow and scattershot. We might get started on something then sputter. Or we might do something well for a time but not make deep changes.

---

[12] Goleman, Daniel. *Emotional Intelligence: Why It Can Matter More than IQ.* Bantam, 2005

Let me give you an example of how intentionality plays out in my life. One of the questions I get most often is "how do you manage everything on your plate?" At the time of this writing, I am a full-time college professor, and I own two businesses—a leadership development/consulting company and a hot sauce company, which I'm in the processing of selling. I am married with two kids, 7 and 10. It's absolutely critical to me that I am present, accountable, and "all-in" at home. In other words, I refuse to be highly successful in my career but absent at home. Most would agree that I have a lot going on. At the very least, I have a lot that I am responsible for, that I take ownership over. Do I balance everything well, let alone perfectly, all the time? Definitely not. Are there times and seasons where I'm killing it at work but feel a bit absent, like I've missed things at home? Definitely.

But when people ask me "how do you do it all?" I always tell them "I'm intentional." I know, that sounds vague and unhelpful. It sounds like a platitude. But it's true and absolutely does the best job I can think of at describing how I "do it all." And the truth is, doing it all or even doing a lot well is much more art than science. Yes, there are "time management" techniques and systems out there, along with programs and apps and many other things you can use. I use a variety of tools to differing degrees in my life. That is the science (and systems) side of it. But for me, there's an art to it that I find on balance and over time, to be where the magic happens. Side note: one of the best books on time management I've ever read is Oliver Burkeman's *Four Thousand Weeks*.[13] Get it and *make time* to go through it, slowly.

---

[13] Burkeman, Oliver. *Four Thousand Weeks: Time Management for Mortals.* McMillan, 2021.

To help firm it up a bit, I want you to **think of intentionality as** *setting your mind to something*. You give it a focus. You think about it a lot. You work on it. You pay attention to it. Your "something" or your "it" could be anything. If "work-life balance" or "work-life integration" (which I prefer) is important to me—and it is—then I set my mind to it. I think about it a lot.

What does that look like, in practice? I use questions like the ones below to filter decisions about work, business, and family opportunities. Note: the questions you use will and should vary depending on your life, seasons, and rhythms. Think about what yours may look like, to the extent they are predictable. For example, as a professor with two school-aged kids at home, my life happens in semesters. I experience fairly intense sprints to the finish line between August and early December, with 3-4 weeks "off" at Christmas. Then, I sprint from January to early May when I shift to online teaching most of the time for the summer. Technically, I am not obligated to Belmont in the months of June and July, so I don't have to worry about checking in and being at work if I don't want to. I teach online in the summers, however, so it behooves me (and my students!) to remain connected. Bottom line, think of your patterns and then craft some questions to help guide you. Some of mine are—

- If I say yes to this, what will I have to say no to, at home?

- If I take one hour to attend _____, what has to give, at home?

- If I'd like to take Friday off for a daytrip with my family, how can I manage my time wisely Monday-Thursday?

- What are the big projects I need to accomplish between January and April so we can have a fun and relaxing summer?

- What does it look like to give the best of me to my students AND be present with my family when I get home?

As you can see from the above questions, I don't have all the answers about how to do it all. At the end of the day, part of leading myself well is admitting I'm not sure about everything. There are weeks and months and seasons of life where I feel like I'm killing it at home but my work slips. And plenty that goes the other direction—work is great but I feel like I haven't seen my kids all week. Any working parents saying amen to that? The main point though is that I'm intentional. I'm continuously and consciously setting my mind to trying to integrate and balance things. But, as you can see from my example, it takes *vulnerability* to admit that and work on it. And it's there that we turn next.

Personalize It

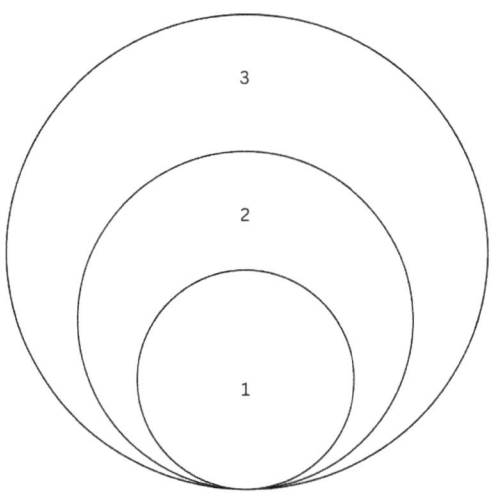

Fill in the 3 Levels of Leadership model using the following as guidelines and suggestions. For each level, I encourage you to describe and evaluate.

- Level three—write down the big projects, initiatives, tasks, etc., you are responsible for and rate your effectiveness on each from 1-10 (1 being least effective)

- Level two—who are the people you lead? If you are not a people leader, who are your colleagues close to you whom you influence, whether you realize it or not? How effective are you at leading/influencing others (1-10)?

- Level one, what are your "self-leadership" goals and tasks you want to work on? Where do you stand now (1-10)?

SECTION II

Be Open

In this section we look at four practices to help you be more open and honest about your needs for development and areas on which to improve. These four practices, with a chapter devoted to each, comprise part one of the Model of Authentic Leader Development: be vulnerable, be authentic, reflect, and project. If you're ready, I'll meet you on the next page!

4

Be Vulnerable

We appreciate people who are vulnerable. After all, nobody likes a know-it-all. Don't we like it when someone just admits, "I'm not sure"? Well, as it turns out, yes and no.

As leaders, let's be honest, sometimes we're afraid vulnerability will be seen as weakness or incompetence. Leaders are paid to act, to decide. And as we saw in Chapter 2, as we age, we move from questioning to (supposedly) knowing, especially as we move up the ranks and gain more experience in life and business. Most of us got to the point we're at in our careers because of our knowledge, our expertise. Most might even refer to us as "subject-matter experts." **So, the question then becomes, how can someone be knowledgeable and vulnerable?**

As it turns out, balance here, as in most areas of life, is key. Leaders need to be competent and seen as such so that team members know they can be counted on to provide correct decisions, execute, and offer support and guidance. Especially if one is new to a team or newly in a leadership role, it can damage a leader's credibility to display too much vulnerability early on, especially depending on how the vulnerability is framed. For instance, a leader who finds herself at a loss of how to tackle a complex problem without framing it as a problem for the entire team to solve will no doubt suffer a hit to her credibility.

Vulnerability simply harnesses the power of one of the most potent and empowering phrases we need in our vocabulary—I don't know.[14] Importantly, what needs to come next, and this is where framing is key, is *but let's find out.* In this subtle framing, leaders avoid the know-it-all air *and* empower others to help solve problems.

In the context of leader development in particular, vulnerability comes through in a leader's willingness to work on himself alongside his followers. Vulnerable leaders can be heard saying things such as, "Here's what I'm working on," "Let's work on this together," and "One thing that I can struggle with is…" The simple fact of the matter is that it's extremely unlikely that followers will put forth their best effort to develop and work on themselves if they don't see their leaders doing the same.

I recall a time when I was leading a training workshop for a large company on the topic of delivering effective feedback. As I was working through some concepts and core practices for how to do it well, I was distracted by some commotion at one of the tables where two leaders seemed annoyed and frustrated. When I asked them what was going on, a leader boldly said, "I know this stuff is important, but our leaders need to

---

[14]   Engelberg, Moshe. *The Incredible Power of Saying 'I Don't Know.* Inc. com, 2022.

be in here." This exchange has always stuck with me because, whether accurate, fair, or an exaggeration, these leaders were simply communicating that they didn't feel that their leaders were willing to put in the time to learn what they wanted their people to learn. This instance also underscores the importance of follow-up between leaders in a training session and their leaders where vulnerability can be shared. Essentially, an exchange of ideas around "What were your most important takeaways" and "Those are things I have worked hard on throughout my career as well" can go a long way toward successful leader development, both for leaders and their people.

With that backdrop on vulnerability provided, let's explore some ways to put vulnerability into practice. A helpful place to start is with our feelings, as feelings are a place where our vulnerability is often on full display. Chances are you're familiar with the phrase, "I'm feeling vulnerable today," or its opposite, "I feel invincible today!"

To firm this up some for you and give you a way to practice vulnerability to your advantage, I bring in a framework popularized by the brilliant and insightful Daniel Pink in his book *The Power of Regret*. Pink points out that feelings aren't something we regard as helpful when it comes to executing, solving problems, etc., so we often ignore them. Instead, we value thinking because thinking helps us in our doing—"we think in order to act."[15] Instead, Pink notes a different and healthier viewpoint—feeling is for thinking. Then, that thinking can aid us in acting. If we put it together, therefore, it goes like this:

Feeling → Thinking → Doing

---

[15]   Pink, Daniel. *The Power of Regret: How Looking Backward Moves Us Forward*. Riverhead Books, 2022, p. 52.

Pink isn't writing in the context of leadership development specifically, but I see much value in this approach for how you work on your leadership and develop as a leader. In the next chapter we'll see how we can turn negative events into positive learning opportunities. For now, **learning to be vulnerable and allowing our feelings to be a catalyst for growth offers a helpful starting point.** For instance, one of the most common issues I run into as an educator, trainer, and coach, and something we've all personally felt, if we're being honest, is imposter syndrome. Let's say you're in a new role, perhaps recently promoted and now lead a team of four. You often find yourself being asked questions to which you're unsure of the answers. On top of that, you're now being asked to develop others while also being made fully aware of the need to sharpen your own skills so you can meet the needs of your team, lead well, and execute.

If we break down the inevitable experience of imposter syndrome using the feeling-thinking-doing method, it would go something like the following. As I'm breaking this down, see if you can relate to what I share. Better yet, do a similar breakdown for recent feelings of vulnerability you've had using the Personalize It section at the back of the chapter. As you'll see, when using the feeling-thinking-doing method, you can do it productively or unproductively. Let's look at both.

Imposter Syndrome

Feeling	Thinking	Doing
Inadequate	I can't do this	Withdraw
Dumb	I can't answer their questions	Avoid their questions
Ill-equipped		Give them BS answers
Lacking capacity	I'm giving them BS answers	Fake it, false bravado
Like a fraud		Avoid leadership roles
	They're going to find me out	
	I'll get demoted soon	

If we're being honest (vulnerable!), we've all been here before. What you notice is that in the first, unproductive method outlined above, we really don't use our feelings much at all. Instead, we get stuck there in the sense that we let them guide our actions—"I always trust my feelings." Instead, **we must get to the point where we honor our feelings and then use them to reflect, thereby sharpening ourselves.** When we do, it might go something like this:

Feeling	Thinking	Doing
Inadequate	Where do these feelings come from? Are they valid?	Reading, learning
Dumb		Listening to podcasts
Ill-equipped	When was the last time I felt like this and made it?	Getting training
Lacking capacity		Getting a coach
Like a fraud		Talking to my team
	What can I learn to help me with this?	Working together to solve problems more
	Who can I talk to about this?	Empowering them to find answers
	Who can help me?	
	How can I empower my team?	

What do you notice about the second example? One thing I hope you see is that you insert questions to help you process what those feelings mean. **What have those feelings come to teach you?** You don't shove them aside, but you also don't trust them 100%.

If you're thinking about how to process something using this format, don't get hung up on what goes where in terms of the different boxes/columns. The main point is to learn to listen to your feelings but don't stop there. Let feelings of hurt, inadequacy, anger, regret, etc., cause you to reflect and *think*. Then, **let your thinking drive you to more productive, effective, and smarter actions.**

To consider another example, briefly, let's say you sat down with your boss for a performance review, and you didn't get the feedback you wanted or thought you deserve. You might have even said some things that you wish you hadn't, or perhaps your tone wasn't one you're proud of. You might be feeling some or all of anger, disappointment, hurt, confusion, and embarrassment. Pick one and study it. For example, if you're confused by the feedback, study it (think) and ascertain what it was due to. Was it your execution? Your communication? Your team leadership? Lack of accountability? Chances are you might have talked about some of these with your boss on the spot, but upon further reflection, one action might be a follow-up with your boss to ask these further questions, get more feedback, and to gameplan a path forward (i.e., feedforward). At that point, you can move to action, knowing better how to tackle the challenges based on how you felt and the time you spent processing.

I also want to point out another potent use of the feeling-thinking-doing framework: its promise for you as a developer of others. After all, every tool, method, and framework in this book can and should be used for your self-development and in the development of others! Let's take the previous example and change the roles—you are the boss, and a direct report doesn't react the way you would have wanted him to. You can encourage him to take the feedback, and his reaction, and reflect on it. You can also use your position to help him process it and map out a path forward.

In this chapter, we learned that vulnerability, although valued by most, is difficult to practice. As leaders, we are paid to think, to decide, to execute. We feel that vulnerability can compromise our competence. However, I hope what you read challenged those assumptions by showing how being vulnerable and specifically using your feelings productively helps you think better and ultimately, execute better.

Personalize It

Part I: Description

Take the Feeling → Thinking → Doing table below and complete it for yourself based on a recent experience. For maximum effectiveness, pick a concrete example or situation, such as the ones highlighted above.

Feeling	Thinking	Doing

Part II: Reflection

What are your personal takeaways from this exercise?

What does it show you about yourself, the situation, etc.?

What does it teach you about how you can use your emotions?

What can you do differently next time when similar situations arise?

5

Be Authentic: The Good, Bad, Ugly

A s we learned in the previous chapter, vulnerability, when practiced well, helps us bridge the gap between our feelings and emotions. Vulnerability is also used in another critical process: authenticity. To be authentically you, you must show the truest version of yourself, which inevitably includes those vulnerable feelings.

Authenticity has become quite a buzzword of late in the business world. It feels like with public levels of trust on the decline for more sectors of society[16], **people just appreciate people who are the real deal**. In the context of leadership and leader development, one could find a slew of definitions out there. For our purposes, recall that authenticity is simply

---

[16] Edelman Trust Institute. *2024 Edelman Trust Barometer Global Report*. 2023.

seeing yourself as a work in progress.[17] I find that in developing leaders, that's the most honest, refreshing, and frankly useful way to define it. As you can hopefully see, labeling yourself as a work in progress takes vulnerability, which means you're on the path toward using your emotions to think better and act better (see Chapter 4).

Authenticity in the form of seeing yourself as a work in progress is potent because when you view yourself that way, you're simply more open to development. This viewpoint, in turn, unlocks so many of the other processes we've covered thus far. For instance, back to the examples from Chapter 1, if you're attending a training seminar or are being coached, you're much more likely to gain from the experience and learn in a sustained way when you believe you have something to learn.

Duh, right? Not so fast. It's all too common for people to be engaged in formal learning but simply take what they learn and file it away with the things they already know and do. This happens for one of two reasons, sometimes both. First, it's simply a matter of information processing. Our brains are finite, and one of the ways we process what can seem like an infinite amount of information is by filing things into familiar categories and digestible units.[18] When you work and handle situations, especially over long periods of time (e.g., your career), those situations build patterns in your brain via neuropathways.[19] As we encounter subsequent

---

[17]   H. Barra, "The Authenticity Paradox," *Emotional Intelligence: Authentic Leadership.* 2018.

[18]   Portianyi, Anton. *What is Information Processing Theory: Using it in Your Corporate Training.* Academy Ocean, 2023.

[19]   Green, C.S., & Bavelier, D. *Exercising your Brain: A Review of Human Brain Plasticity & Training-Induced Learning.* Psychology and Aging, 2008.

situations, those experiences get put into those same channels as ways of handling things, akin to how we can take a drive home on a familiar route but seemingly do so subconsciously. Our brains are efficient and just plain good at processing like that.

The trouble comes when the content and practices being taught offer a new way of tackling challenges or handling difficult situations, but we miss it because we're not authentic enough to recognize, let alone agree, that perhaps what we're learning is a new way of seeing things. **A leader who is a perpetual work in progress simply doesn't have that trouble and sees skills and content for the opportunity they offer to think differently about one's leadership and challenges.**

Whereas the first reason has neuroscience backing it, the second is more about our psychology and specifically our egos. Put bluntly, we might just not think we need the new info, let alone new ways of doing things. After all, that requires us to think differently and, by definition, requires us to start wearing different pathways in our brain. It requires honest reflection to know what you know and what you don't know. As you progress in your career and your leadership experience, chances are you got to where you are because of your knowledge, your expertise. Well, authenticity and seeing yourself as a work in progress demands that you put that aside and look for ways to grow, question, and develop. Again, it requires vulnerability to ask questions, a task that's especially difficult when it's your personal development involved.

One of the challenges with authenticity is it can be difficult to know how to put it into practice. Seeing yourself as a "work in progress" might sound good, but what does that look like? A helpful way to incorporate the work in progress mindset in life is found through a "lifespan" perspective on leadership development.[20] Central to the lifespan perspective are "triggers" that are known to spur growth in leaders. Traditionally, "triggers" connote something negative, but an authentic development viewpoint widens the frame to include positive events. Let's explore both here to help show how you can learn to view yourself authentically, as a work in progress in how you process the bad and good experiences in life.

First, consider the negative experiences you've had. I encourage you to pause as you're reading this and list a few that come to mind. These could be personal or professional. Here are some common negative experiences to consider:

- Severe illness.

- Death of a loved one.

- Job loss.

- Being passed over for a promotion.

- Being demoted.

- Not getting a job for which you thought you were a sure fit.

- Losing a business deal.

- Having to lay off a team member (or entire team).

When bad things happen, or things don't happen the way you want or think they should, how do you respond? I have a pastor friend who loves to say, "treat your past as a school,

---

[20] Fred Luthans and Bruce Avolio. "Authentic Leadership Development," *Positive Organizational Scholarship: Foundations of a New Discipline.* 2003.

not a prison." That's it. Excellent, wise advice for life and your leader development in particular. I once knew someone who was demoted at a stage of life when one assumes it's onward and upward until retirement. Instead, in his early 50s, it went the opposite direction. He spent more than five years dwelling on that bitterly. It colored his interactions, his choices not to apply for other opportunities, and so many other things. The response he chose was bitterness. Plain and simple. I'm not saying it's easy to avoid that; I'm saying our response is a choice.

Research on resilience, which by definition, involves bouncing back from negative experiences, is clear that what differentiates people who show resilience from those who don't lies in asking "why" versus "what". When bad things happen, it's ok to explore *why* for a short period. Some questions you can ask include:

- Why did that happen?

- Why did _____ get promoted over me?

- Why did _____ have to get sick and pass away?

- Why didn't I get that job that I thought was a sure thing?

- Why didn't I even get called for an interview for that job I thought was a sure thing?

- Why did _____ criticize me in front of the whole team?

The important thing in learning from negative experiences is asking *what*, as in:

- What am I going to do now?

- What can this teach me to help me get better, smarter, more efficient, more patient, etc.?

- What will I do differently?

- What can _____ (person who got promoted over you) teach me about how to _____ (whatever job, task, role) better/differently?

Let me share an extended personal example that you might be able to relate to. Several years ago, while I was on the job market for the role I currently occupy, I applied for a position for which I thought I was a slam dunk. The fit with the role was spot on (so I thought) and it was at a prestigious university. Not only that, but we had family close by the university. I remember saying to my department chair, who had agreed to write a recommendation letter for me, "If I could have written the job description, I'm not sure I would have written a better one to suit me." He agreed, and what made it more of a slam dunk in my mind, was that my department chair knew the search committee chair from their days in college. Surely his written recommendation combined with his verbal endorsement combined with my perfect fit for the role would make it an easy path. Well, as the saying goes, "we plan, God laughs."

About a month after applying, it had been crickets, so I emailed the search chair to see what the deal was and check for any updates. She informed me that they had just started inviting candidates to campus for in-person interviews. My stomach dropped and I literally shed some tears. This obviously meant I wasn't a finalist and not only that, but I didn't even get an initial interview. I faced the double hurt of not only not getting the job I thought was perfect for me, but my pride was in the toilet because I didn't even get a screening interview. Admittedly, I was in *why* mode for a few days after that. But after a short time, I decided to email the chair for some feedback. Based on what she shared, I learned that it wasn't a great fit after all based on what they teach in their program and where they were heading, and what I teach, and I took stock of what I needed to add to my knowledge base to remain competitive in the marketplace. In short, I got answers to the *why* and the *what*.

Why keeps us in the past; *what* moves us forward. Importantly, *what* still honors the past, but it learns from it and helps us get better. I'm not saying this will be easy but try it. You'll have a space to do this at the end of the chapter but take a negative experience you noted at the start of this section and pose some *what* questions from the list above. There's a lot to gain and virtually nothing to lose from flipping the script on your negative experiences. And, thankfully, most of our disappointments involve other people, who might just be willing to share, at the very least, *why* things didn't work out like we wanted. Then it's up to us to decide what to do about it.

However, negative trigger events are only half the story. We can learn a lot from positive events as well, provided we have the right mindset about and orientation toward those events. In my experience, people are much more likely to learn from negative experiences and don't spend much time thinking about how they can get better from positive events. It makes sense. After all, we're supposed to get better after bad stuff. Correct what's wrong, compensate, etc., right? Yes, but there's so much more in life to learn from, and hopefully in the end your life includes more on the positive side of the ledger.

Take note of some recent positive events in your life you can learn from. They might include things such as:

- Voluntarily changing careers.

- Starting a brand-new project for your boss (could also be negative!).

- A career milestone or transition (e.g., promotion, retirement).

- Working with a new colleague who brings new energy to your work.

- A new committee assignment.

- Listening to an insightful podcast.

- Reading an insightful book.

- Attending a training and development event.

- Meeting a significant other who has a different worldview.

I encourage you to apply many of the same questions in both the *why* and the *what* sections above to your positive experiences. Some of them might be obvious, like when you read a good book or listen to a good podcast and make note of takeaways you want to apply to your leadership. Others might be less obvious in terms of our tendency to reflect. For instance, reflecting deeply on why you chose to change careers can be insightful and help you firm up your commitments, avoid future negative experiences (ones that should be avoided), and provide you with a stockpile of advice to share with future generations. I find myself in this position often as an advisor and educator, as in when a student asks me why I chose to leave Marquette if I was happy there. Most often, however, the questions are more general, as in, "How do I know when to start looking for a new role?" I've just found that it's good to have reflected on my own experiences so I'm ready to engage those around me in those important discussions. You don't have to have all the answers but some thoughtful reflection on the front end can go a long way in helping others.

The biggest obstacle for most of us in reflecting on the good is taking the time to do so. Notice I didn't say *having* the time. We just don't take, or better yet, *make* the time to do it. I can't give you more hours in the day. I can only challenge you to start prioritizing reflection in your day—and your weeks, months, quarters, and beyond. It needs to be part of your busy. My hope for you is that you find some tools here in this chapter and beyond that will help you incorporate simple, doable methods into your busy schedule.

Small and Large Questions

At the start of nearly every training workshop I lead I ask some version of the question, "What do you hope to get out of this workshop? Or "What skills would you like to improve in _____ [topic of workshop]?" If participants have given the workshop any forethought whatsoever, they can usually answer it on some level. If the workshop is on effective communication, they might respond with "being more assertive" or "I'd like to be able to give better feedback." Questions like these are critical for leader development because they help to set intentions, to give the leader something to aim for. In a way, they paint a picture of what success looks like for our time together. Essentially, it gives them a sense of, "At the end of this workshop, it will be a success if I can _____ more effectively."

These are important questions and trainings, or any leadership development effort for that matter, should include them. But these are also examples of what you could call "small" questions.

If we did a dive into human behavior development and in particular, psychology, we would find an important distinction between "small" and "large" questions. The psychologist James Hollis writes about these two types of questions often.[21] For Hollis, one thing that can explain happiness, or lack thereof, in the second half of life, is whether someone has been intentional about asking "large questions." For most of us, we spend time thinking about things that are, indeed, important to us as we go through life; what our jobs/careers will entail, whom we will spend our time with, be it our friends or spouse, and whether we saved enough for retirement.

To be clear, these *are* important questions. How we spend our lives at work, our life partners, and being secure financially, of course play a big role in our happiness. But the important thing is whether those are the *only* questions we ask. For instance, a job that pays well, without regard to whether it serves people, makes a difference, and is personally fulfilling, is bound to leave one dissatisfied, perhaps even chronically. Other large questions in the context of life include, *why am I here? In service to what? What truly matters to me? How do I find my path?* In a religious context, a large question that personally drives my work is, *does what I'm doing bring glory to God?*

---

[21]   Hollis, James. *Finding Meaning in the Second Half of Life: How to Finally, Really Grow Up.* Avery, 2006.

54

I contend that **in the context of leader development, most of what we do is ask small questions.** What skills do I want to improve on, how can _____ skill help me lead my team better, how can I make sure my "soft" skills keep up with my core, technical skills?

Again, these are all important questions. But my question for you is, are they the only questions you're asking?

If so, **I challenge you to be intentional about asking large questions.** Many of these might be personal, and even coming up with the questions takes some reflection, but some examples include,

- Who do I want to become, as a person, as a leader?

- What do I want people to see, as a result of my skill development?

- What do I want to be the impression people get of me when I leave the room?

- How do I want to "show up" around others?

- How am I using the platforms God has given me to serve well?

- What am I doing with the influence I'm given?

- If these development efforts are successful, how will my development and advancement improve people's lives?

As you begin the process of asking those types of questions, they help you set deeper intentions. Deeper intentions are more likely to lead to authentic behaviors and sustained change. Then, as you begin to learn new skills, about which you've undoubtedly considered those "small" questions we talked about earlier, you can place those changes in a larger context. In other words, *why* makes all the difference.

So, next time you're approaching a training, seminar, workshop, or coaching engagement, be sure to start with these large questions. Even just starting with one question can lead to sustained, even *large* changes.

Personalize It

Part I: Triggers

Identify ONE positive event ("trigger") you can apply to your leadership development

What can this event/situation teach you to make you better?

Identify ONE negative event ("trigger") you can apply to your leadership development

What can this event/situation teach you to make you better?

Part II: Small → Large Questions

Using the examples above as a starting point, write one small question and connect it to a large question to help you place your leadership development in a larger context.

Write your answer to your large question below to help you identify a larger "why" for one of your development goals.

6

Reflect

Humor me for a second and do a quick, honest audit. Generally speaking, how often would you say you spend reflecting? Reflecting on your life, on your happiness and fulfillment, on your job performance, on your communication, on your leadership? Is this a weekly practice? Do you do it monthly? How do you reflect informally throughout the day, formally at the end of the week in a journal or other reflection tool? In my experience, in a moment of total honesty, most leaders would say *not very often, not much at all, or hardly ever.*

I get it. As I've said before, you get paid to decide, to execute. It's hard to justify time to slow down and reflect. Broadly speaking, people are largely unreflective and lack awareness of just how little they reflect. Read that again. To state it another way, **we aren't aware that we aren't aware.**

Dr. Tasha Eurich, organizational psychologist and *New York Times* bestselling author, reports that even though most people think they're self-aware, only 10-15% of people actually are, based on core self-awareness practices (e.g., journaling, seeking feedback).[22] Her research shows that several things hinder self-awareness including experience, which can lead to false confidence about our performance. Power is another hindrance because as you move up into leadership roles, there are simply fewer people above you to give feedback and those below you might fear giving it.

Whatever the reasons and hindrances, self-awareness remains a critical skill, a "meta-skill," as Eurich calls it. Self-awareness is "meta" because it's a practice that leads to success in many areas of leadership. For example, it's one thing to learn a concrete skill such as active listening. It's an entirely different thing, however, to learn about it, practice it, and reflect on how you're progressing along the path to be a better listener. To go a step further, I contend that efforts to develop without reflection are doomed to fail. Indeed, I can teach you an active listening technique in a classroom or coaching setting, but until you try it, see how it's going, and make some changes based on you, your style, your experiences, it's unlikely to sustain.

Although there are many ways for a leader to be self-aware and reflect (e.g., gathering feedback), self-appraisal is one of the most readily available methods. After all, all you really need is, well, you. But there's a catch. **How you reflect is as important, if not more so, than whether you reflect.** An argument could be made that any reflection is better than none, except that studies have shown that highly

---

[22] Talesnik, Dana. *Eurich Explores Why Self-Awareness Matters.* NIH Record, 2009.

introspective people are actually less self-aware and report lower well-being.[23] The main reason lies in *how* we reflect. The crucial factor in self-reflection is the types of questions we ask when we reflect. As it turns out, asking *why* something happened (e.g., *why did I fly off the handle in that one-on-one meeting?*) doesn't work as well because we tend to jump to incorrect conclusions about the reason. We might, for instance, attribute the behavior to a fatal flaw within ourselves or the other person. We might think we're not cut out for the job, or that the other person just isn't teachable.

A better method of self-reflection is to be more objective by asking *what* questions. Put simply, the more objective we can be, the better off we are. Questions like the one below can be more effective

- What was said and done to cause that reaction?

- What can I do differently to avoid this similar outcome?

- What similar situations have caused this reaction?

When it comes to self-reflection, one of the most powerful practices I've used with thousands of leaders is Mental Replay. The Mental Replay practice is based on what high-performing athletes, especially in team sports, are known for—watching a lot of film. If you're a football fan, you might know that after a series, you'll see players on the sidelines looking at a tablet. What are they doing on those tablets? They're watching their and others' performance

---

[23] Grant, Anthony, Franklin, John, & Langford, Peter. "The Self-Reflection and Insight Scale: A New Measure of Private Self-Consciousness. *Social Behavior and Personality*, 2002.

from the previous plays to get a chance to see what happened—good and bad. This allows the players, notably the quarterback, to get an objective viewpoint of their performance, and their behavior. Of course, the goal is to take that viewpoint, that feedback, and make changes to it in subsequent series. They might learn to spot in-game tendencies in different defensive packages or how to recognize disguised blitzes so they can adjust next time out. They don't have the luxury of pausing the game in real time to study, so they must count on their reflection to give them new data to use in the heat of play.

So it goes with leader reflection. The rub is, when reflecting on our behavior, our communication, outside of recording ourselves giving a speech or leading a meeting, it's just hard to get the "film."

Enter—Mental Replay. The Mental Replay tool can be found in the online companion site[24] for the book, but in brief, this tool allows you to get a somewhat objective viewpoint on your behavior and use that data to action plan. If possible, I recommend having a copy of the tool in front of you for reference. Here's a quick rundown on how it could work along with an example.

The goal is to use the tool following any communication situation—a presentation, a meeting, a 1-1 conversation with a direct report (or your spouse!). The situation and conversation could have gone well, it could have gone poorly—it doesn't matter. What matters is that you have a situation to reflect on. Immediately after the situation, or as soon as possible, sit down and complete the worksheet.

The following example is a hypothetical situation based on a common challenge in my world. For a bit of context,

---

[24]   www.authenticleaderdevelopment.com/resources/toolkit

in a former role as a director of a graduate program, my job was to ensure students meet their requirements to graduate, including taking their required courses and finishing their final, culminating project, for which they choose either an academic thesis or professional project. A thesis is an academically targeted project, whereas a professional project is targeted at a specific professional organization (e.g., a business). This example is about a graduate student working in the final stages of completing a thesis project, confused on requirements to finish the project with revisions. In short, she thought she was across the finish line on her project but had significant revisions to make per one of her committee members, which she didn't know was a possibility. To personalize this for you and your leadership, you might find it helpful to think of a situation where an employee didn't meet expectations on a project, resulting in a missed deadline, substandard work, or unsatisfied clients.

Step one is to explore the situation as objectively as you can, hence the camera icon on the worksheet. You'll want to simply describe what happened:

1. Situation

   • Describe what happened—Had a conversation with Cathy about her thesis options. We made decisions about her next steps.

   • Results, outcomes—She decided she will stick with the thesis option and complete her revisions rather than changing to a capstone project option.

In step two, you do some reflection using three prompts including thinking, feeling, and saying/doing.

2. Reflection

- What was I thinking—Did I cause her confusion? What role did I play in her confusion? Is she taking enough responsibility in the matter?

- What I was feeling—Students are quick to blame others. I was frustrated that there wasn't a lot of time before graduation for her to make revisions.

- What I said and did—I told her she was looking at the wrong guidelines (professional project instead of thesis). I stood my ground, offered her support, pointed her to the correct guidelines (thesis).

In step three, you'll mine for insights by considering habits, lessons, and takeaways.

3. Insights

- Habits, patterns—I tend to over-accept responsibility and over-apologize.

- Lessons, takeaways—Be careful not to take so much ownership that it lets people off the hook.

In step four, this is where you game plan for next time.

4. Action

- Next time I will—Set up a more rigorous process. Establish a timeline with each thesis advisor and conduct at least one check-in with the student per semester.

Here are just a few words of advice on using the Mental Replay for maximum effectiveness. One tendency that all of us busy people have when we reflect, if we reflect, is we tend to go from situation to action. In other words, something happens, we think about it a bit, then decide what to do differently next time. It's not wrong, necessarily, but it's incomplete because it misses critical components—reflection and insight. **Something needs to come between the situation and what will happen next time,** much in the same way that the quarterback will consider how he responded to the movements and action of the other players before deciding what to do. Bottom line: don't skip the middle two steps. When you combine the "objective" perspective via steps one and four with the more subjective introspection of reflection and insights, it's a potent activity. It will simply give you a better shot at sustaining changes long term because you get a more complete picture.

Additionally, I recommend you complete the Mental Replay over consistent experiences over time. For example, if you have a standing Monday morning meeting with your team, conduct a replay after each meeting for four weeks. Doing this will give you a consistent sample against which to compare and map out a plan for moving forward. Finally, as with any other tools and techniques you find in this book, don't go it alone. Share your results with your team, your colleagues, your friends, your spouse—anyone—as you work through it. In fact, I recommend you conduct the Replays together. Speaking from experience, it makes a great team-building experience to work through it together. **You get to grow together and share in team vulnerability, two potent factors in your personal growth journey.**

Pause Points

As you read the above about how to conduct a Mental Replay, you might be thinking, *there's no way I can take the time to do that. I'm too busy!* If you thought that, I get it, and I respect it. I would challenge you to prioritize it anyway, but I also want to offer you simpler, and quicker, ways to reflect during your busy day.

Thus, I recommend taking "pause points" throughout the day. To give credit where credit is due, the idea behind this practice comes from Dr. Mark Jones, creator of Be with Jesus 365. Although Dr. Jones's organization is dedicated to helping people be more intentional in their walks with Jesus and faith journeys more broadly, the lesson and practice holds promise for anyone being intentional about their development.

Pause points are simple, short exercises designed to get you out of the daily grind and bring your attention back to where you want it to be—in other words, what you're wanting to be intentional about. Let's explore what this might look in my life, and I encourage you to consider the same for yourself. In a given week in a given semester, I'm pulled in 100 different directions. As a husband and father, my wife and kids need me to be present. Of course, I want to always be the best version of myself; that's where my intentions are. At work, when I'm teaching 3-4 classes in a semester, and advising, I have 70-100 students whose educational experience depends largely on me, my preparation, my engagement in the classroom, and my support when they need help on school stuff and sometimes life stuff. And that's just my full-time job. I'm also running a consulting and training practice, so I have client partners who depend on me for their leadership development and guidance. To keep it short, suffice it to say, I can get in the weeds of "getting stuff done." Gotta pay the bills, right? That's what I tell myself. But if I'm not careful, it's just too easy to get lost in trees and miss the forest. The forest is where my sights should remain, or at least be brought back to, often. That's where pause points come in.

At 4-5 points throughout the day, I can simply pause from the hustle and bring my attention back to the big picture. My big picture, the "why," is to bring my best self to every encounter with others so I can encourage and develop. In short, I don't want to miss opportunities God has blessed me with to make a difference in someone's life. And I have lots of them, if I'll just slow down and pay attention.

A pause point could be a prayer, 5 minutes of silence, 10 deep breaths, or repeating a mantra. It's anything you can use to detach for a brief moment and bring your attention back, to zoom out from the immediate, pressing concerns in front of you. Pause points are also handy for helping us as we move in between different contexts—from a classroom to a meeting, from training a big group of leaders to coaching someone one-on-one. Different situations have different rhythms, tones, and expectations. Stephan Rechtschaffen, in his book *Timeshifting*, explores this in depth, noting that because of the different rhythms found from one setting to another, if we don't train ourselves to "shift" – down or up – our communication and overall effectiveness is minimized.[25] This process is known as "rhythmic entrainment," analogous to how you tap your foot to a beat faster or slower depending on the rhythm of a song. If you've ever gone from a lighthearted, easy meeting to a serious one-on-one, then

---

[25] Rechtschaffen, Stephan. *Timeshifting: Creating More Time to Enjoy Your Life.* Crown, 1997.

you know how important it is to "downshift" to prepare for that meeting.

Pause points can be helpful throughout your day but also before important meetings and even before you go inside your house after a long day. In fact, spending 2-3 minutes in your car, in your driveway or garage, can be a simple but effective way to shift into the rhythms of home life—up or down. At the time of this writing, my kids are 7 and 10, so no matter how crazy my day is, most of the time it feels like an up-shift when I get in the door. In other words, no matter how tired I am or how crazy my day was, kids always seem to bring more energy than I have left. Can I get an amen from parents out there? And I don't know about you, but I still want to bring my best self through the door with me when I get home. Kids need to know that hard work is tiring, *and* they need to know that they're a priority. Beyond that, taking a pause point before going in can help avoid arguments and fights with your significant other, as many report that the first 15 minutes after arriving home are some of the most challenging of the day.[26] In summary, **as you can see, pause points can help at work and at home**.

Data Mining

One challenge to developing—yourself and others—is knowing what to work on, what to look for. How do you know when you're not showing up as the person or leader you'd like to be? You might have an inkling that you need to be more assertive, but can you recall a recent example where you lacked assertiveness but needed it? To close out

---

[26] Batista, Ed. *How Not to Fight with your Spouse When you Get Home from Work.* Harvard Business Review, 2016.

this chapter, I offer you an additional, simple technique to help address the challenge of recalling examples and knowing what to look for.

I recommend you practice "data mining." Data scientists search large data sets (e.g., news articles, social media posts) to look for patterns and trends. The goal is to turn their findings into insights and predictions audiences such as business can use to make decisions and act in the future.

If you stop and think about it, as leaders and communicators, our worlds offer a steady stream of "datasets" we can search. If you're interacting with people at all at work, you're emailing, talking on the phone, passing people in the hallway, videoconferencing, giving presentations, holding one-on-ones, attending meetings, and countless other contexts. The data sets are practically endless! Beyond that, each day is a new day, adding wrinkles and complexity to the sets. My encouragement here is to train yourself to mine those data sets so you can spot your own habits, triggers, tendencies, and so on. Put simply, you're going to start being intentional in looking for examples of your areas for development, as well as your strengths.

A word of caution—be sure to balance honest reflection and appraisal with grace. If you're not careful, you'll drive yourself crazy or get paranoid about your own behavior. I just want you to start taking your own development seriously to the point where you work on that while you're working. Just like you (hopefully) focus your attention carefully on what you're doing and the actual work you're evaluated on, start paying attention to you, your communication, how you're leading, etc. It deserves a large part of your attention and intention.

I first heard the term "data mining" in this context from a pastor friend of mine, Brandon (see the Introduction) who was giving a talk at a men's retreat one year. He was focused in that talk on reflecting on one's past to help be better now and prepare for the future. It turns out to be rock solid advice for leaders as well. One quote stood out in particular: "smart men learn from their mistakes. Wise men learn from others' mistakes." Mic drop.

Here, **I'm encouraging you to learn from your mistakes first, but don't forget to pay attention to the positives as well**. As we discussed in Chapter 5, you can learn a lot from positive "triggers" and life moments as well. If you handle a difficult situation with tact and professionalism, keeping your balance effectively, take note. Chances are, there are lessons from that data set you can take with you into others for future situations.

The compounding effect of learning through data mining is that as you learn from your mistakes, it sets you up to help others learn more effectively and authentically. Not to mention, as you learn to pay attention to situations more keenly, you train yourself to spot tendencies in others you want to avoid, hence, learning from others, as wise people do.

Here are some things to consider when you're data mining:

- Time of day—do you react better/worse at certain times of the day?

- People—am I more/less effective with others present?

- Workload—how does a heavy/light workload impact me and how I communicate and lead others?

Beyond some of those general factors, use specific situations and tools to help you data mine. For example, the Mental Replay tool is essentially a data mining tool. It's premised on you reflecting and replaying specific situations to spot patterns and gameplan for the future.

This is one of the longest chapters in the book and that is not by accident. I packed a lot into this chapter, for good reason. Remember, **reflection is a meta-skill**. By being intentional about it, it will lead to success in so many areas of your leadership development and your leadership practice. Whether you reflect using robust tools like Mental Replay or more micro, in-the-moment practices such as pause points and data mining, I promise it will be time well spent.

Personalize It

Conduct a Mental Replay using the guidelines and suggestions above. Visit my online toolkit for a fillable version of the tool. I recommend at least 3-4 replays over 3-4 weeks. (www.authenticleaderdevelopment.com/resources/toolkit)

What are your insights the Mental Replay showed you?

How will you act on what the Mental Replay showed you?

How can you practice "pause points" in your day?

Practice "data mining" throughout the week ahead and then reflect:

What did you notice?

How can you use that info (data)?

7

Project

What do you want to be when you grow up? We've all been asked that, and if you have kids, they've definitely been asked that, most likely by you. As a matter of fact, I'm in my 40s, and sometimes I'm still asking myself that question, but that's a different book entirely! We tend to think a lot about *what* one might want to be (job, profession, etc.), but in leadership, we're missing something big. My question I'd like to ask you here is, *who* do you want to be when you grow up? For the record, if you're already grown up, age-wise, keep in mind, authenticity is all about seeing yourself as a work in progress, so there's always a *who* we're working towards and working to develop.

The word "projection" often carries a negative connotation. In psychological terms, projection is where we take what we're feeling or thinking, and we put that on another—we project it on them. For instance, if I'm feeling insecure or uncertain about something, I might not approach another person because I assume they feel the same way.

However, I want to use projection in a positive sense when it comes to leader development. Put simply, I want you to practice seeing who you'd like to become. **Think of leader development projection as personal vision casting.** Leader projection is also a bridge between reflection and action, hence, its placement here in the book. We'll turn to action next, but in the meantime, in this chapter we explore some ways to think big about who we are and who we'd like to become.

Some basic but important questions to consider at the outset, include: What are you working towards? Better stated, *who* are you working toward becoming? Who do you want to grow into? What type of leader and person are you becoming?

When it comes to projection, there are many things you can project including skills, behaviors, and/or positions. You can look forward and project the types of skills and competencies you know effective leaders need and then work toward that. You can also look ahead and see yourself in a certain role based on what you know is a usual trajectory for your position, based on a role model you admire, or based on a role that you believe would fit your interests and skill set. Still another way to project is by imagining who you'd like to be and work toward that—what we'll call identity-based projection. All types of projections can be helpful, but in the end, identity-based projection will provide more sustainable results and give you a better chance of authentic skill development. In this chapter, I introduce a simple technique for projection you can use in your development. We'll start broad with identity-based projection and work down towards some examples of how you can apply it to skills or positions.

First, a quick primer on identity and its importance for your development. Identity-based projection works better for the same reason that identity-based habit building is more effective. James Clear, in his *New York Times* best-selling book *Atomic Habits*, offers identity-based approaches as one of the key lessons in building effective habits.[27] In short, most people focus on changing outcomes such as losing weight or gaining more customers, or on processes such as going to the gym or investing in more time for customer prospecting. Outcomes and processes are good. But **identity is where the magic happens because it's about you and what you believe.** We start to think more about *who* rather than *what*. I want to *be* a healthy person, not just lose weight. I want to *be* an athlete, rather than just committing to go to the gym. I want to *be* someone who values and cultivates relationships, not just someone who makes one hour of customer prospect calls per day. Do you see the difference?

There are many ways you can use projection in your development, but a good starting place is to conduct what I call a "Leader Gap Analysis." The Leader Gap Analysis is one of the simplest techniques I use in my coaching and leader development trainings and might be the most ubiquitous. Oftentimes I use it at the start of a session to prime the leaders' thinking and set some intentions. Remember back in Chapter 5 when we talked about the importance of setting your intentions at the start of a session? This quick activity helps us do that. Let's run through how to do it then I'll provide some additional tips on when, how often, etc.

To conduct a Leader Gap Analysis, you'll use two simple prompts:

---

[27] Clear, James. *Atomic Habits: Tiny Changes, Remarkable Results.* Avery, 2018.

"The Leader I am Now is…"	"The Leader I'd Like to Be is…"

As you can see, you place the first prompt on the left side, second prompt on the right. The point, of course, is to work to spot a gap between the two. Here's how I instruct leaders and teams to complete it.

First off, don't get hung up on the word "leader." For many of you reading this, you may very well be in a formal leadership position, so this may not be an issue. However, if you're not in a formal leadership role or have any direct reports, you can easily substitute something for "leader." Instead, for example, insert "communicator" in its place. Or, if you have something specific within a skillset like communication, you can drill down and insert "speaker" in place of "leader." Side note: you can also substitute "spouse" or "father" and get plenty of value, but that's a whole different matter!

As far as what goes in the columns, this is where skills or position or identity comes into play. The main thing is you want to be honest in your reflection. We covered vulnerability and authenticity in previous chapters (4 and 5, respectively), but open, honest reflection will serve you well. "Evidence" for where you are now could come from recent things people have told you, formally or informally. For instance, in a recent performance review, your boss might have said you need to work on managing conflict more effectively. Or, less formally, people might often tell you that you don't stand up for yourself often enough. Or, upon introspection and reflection or a after completing a Mental Replay (Chapter 6), you might recognize that your indecisiveness often gets you into trouble, causing people to describe you as wishy-washy.

Whatever the case, put your current behavior/s, current state in the left-hand column.

Next, project where you'd like to be, where you'd like to go, and place that into the right-hand column. Oftentimes, what you project is obvious and flows directly from where you are now, especially if you've identified a concrete skill you'd like to work on. For example, if you identified "indecisive" as where you are now, it might make sense to place "more decisive" in the second column, right? Or perhaps less obvious but still concrete, if you said you tend to be a pushover now, you might project that you'd like to be more assertive. In these cases, the gap is self-evident, and you can get to work building those skills.

Where it can get a little less clear (and fun) is when you aspire to do something or be someone and aren't quite sure how to get there. For instance, I had a training I was conducting recently where we started our day off with this activity, a common occurrence. One of the leaders spent a lot of time on this prompt and I could tell he was chewing on it carefully. In the breakout portion, when they were discussing their results at their tables, he commented, "Right now I'm pretty good at being autonomous and getting stuff done. But there are times when I need to ask my boss for help or I want to give feedback, but I'm not sure how." Think for a second, how would you complete the activity if you were facing that situation? Chances are you have before. There are many directions one could go in to try to bridge that gap. Ultimately, I helped him identify "managing up" as a gap and therefore a skill area we discussed, and he could further develop. When we took his example back to the larger group, it turns out many of his colleagues had similar issues, so I took that opportunity to do a quick primer and activity around managing up.

To offer another example of a less clear-cut gap, I had another training recently around building a leadership brand and professional presence. I used the Gap Analysis activity to kick it off. A woman in the training identified that the team member (she is not a formal people leader) she is now is "knowledgeable" and the team member she'd like to be is "innovative." She reflected that she has a reputation for being a "knower." People come to her for her expertise, and she most often has the answers. Although this isn't necessarily a bad thing, she noted she wants to start being more curious and ensure that she is coming up with innovative and novel approaches instead of a simple copy and paste from one issue to the next. I helped her brainstorm how to bridge the gap and suggested that she have a toolkit of questions she asks about problems or issues that come her way. This would help her pause, think critically, and ensure that she is open and curious about everything. Generally, this example shows how identifying a concrete step can help you bridge the gap, which can be particularly challenging if the gap isn't clear cut.

As the above examples show, the key to first step is to reflect and get descriptive with where you are now and what your goals, aspirations, and desires are in terms of your skills, position, or identity. If you start there, then you can worry about giving the skill or mindset in the gap its proper label, if it's not apparent from doing the exercise in the first place. From my experience doing this activity with hundreds of leaders, the skill area is apparent at least 75% of the time.

To help this sink in a bit more, here's an example of my "Leader Gap Analysis." Here, I'll take you into my own personal development journey so you can see how this could play out. I'll provide two real-time examples.

"The Leader I am Now is…"	"The Leader I'd Like to Be is…"
Pleasing	Challenging/direct
Busy	Available

Take a minute and review my gap analysis here. What would you identify as the actual gap? What goes in there? What are the skill areas I could work on?

Let's assess my two projections above. From my experience, leaders can have a hard time grasping what this might look like—what should go in each column and subsequently, what goes in the gap—so it's time well spent to camp out here.

As I review my results, on the first line, the question to consider is what is the bridge—the gap—between pleasing and challenging/direct? To give you a quick peek behind the curtain of my life, I'm someone who likes for people to get along. I like to leave a situation or conversation knowing that everyone is good with the outcome. I don't like the thought of people being disappointed or feeling badly about me. Mostly, this serves me well because I believe I have a gift for consensus building and collaboration. At worst, however, I worry that I don't challenge people enough or call things out enough when something is amiss. As an educator, this doesn't work well at times. If a student behaves in a way that's unbecoming or unprofessional, for instance, I need to be able to call it out, tactfully. If I'm being honest with you (and myself!), I soften feedback at times for fear of what a student will think. You might take this example and place it in your context to see what it looks like for you. Does a direct report do something wrong or just below average and you let it slide? If so, you can relate to this struggle.

With that background in mind, I've identified "having difficult conversations" as my gap area. I could easily say "being assertive," but I like to get a bit more context specific. This might seem like a distinction without a difference, but it matters. Being assertive can relate to and play out in so many different situations. It could even play out in ways that have little to do with communication. For instance, I could aim to drive more assertively by not always letting people pull in front of me when they wait until the last minute to merge when a lane ends. (This behavior could borderline on aggressiveness, but don't get me started there.) Or, assertiveness could apply in impersonal communication situations, for instance, when I feel like a cashier at Chick fil A rang up something incorrectly or didn't apply a discount properly. If I were tired of being a pushover and just letting things slide by paying a little extra to save the hassle, I could resolve to be more assertive and call it out.

But I encourage you to **be context specific with the gap you spot, based on the time and season you're in**. For me, I'm in a season where it seems that tough conversations are all around me. At the very least, they are situations where people don't automatically see eye-to-eye and it requires some posturing and assertiveness. We're not necessarily fighting or even anticipating a fight, but things just aren't smooth. The bottom line, "having difficult conversations" most accurately captures what I feel I need to hone in on right now. Can you see the difference?

If I look at the second line, as I project into the future, I want to make sure I'm someone who is seen as available, even as I keep a busy schedule. Where does this data point of being seen as "busy" come from? More often than I care to admit, a student will come up to me in the semester, typically near the end and typically because they have been struggling with something, and say something to the effect of, "I wanted to come ask you, but you just seem so busy." At best, they're communicating that they don't want to impose; it's a face-saving act on their part. But at worst, I show up as "I can't be bothered." I'm not ok with this. It's ineffective as an educator who gets paid to help students, and more importantly to me, it's not who I want to be (i.e., my identity). As I alluded to earlier, my identity is rooted in my "why"—I want to use the platforms and voice God has given me to encourage and develop others. I simply can't do that if I "show up" as busy and unavailable.

With that in mind, what goes in the gap there? For me, it's careful planning, and focus and attention management. Notice I didn't say *time* management there. This is beyond our scope here, but in short, since we all have the same amount of time we're working with on this earth, I care more about what I give my attention to and therefore what I focus on. (Two excellent reads on time/attention/focus management are *Four Thousand Weeks* by Oliver Burkeman and *The One Thing* by Gary Keller and Jay Papasan.)

At times, it might very well mean saying "no" and taking things off my plate. In other words, just be less busy. But in many cases, the things I'm giving my attention to are things I've deemed worthy of it, so I need to be more intentional about how I "show up." If I'm in the classroom or otherwise around my students, they need to be my focus, they deserve my attention. I need to hone my presence, maybe try not to talk about the 1000 other things I'm working on in a given month, etc. These can and often are subtle cues to others that our plates are full and there just might not be much room for them.

I conclude this chapter with two final, critical things. First, and most importantly, **when you identify where you**

want to go, you must identify a *why*. For example, it's not enough for me to say I want to be a leader who is available. As we saw in Chapter 3, if we're not intentional about what we're learning and what we're practicing, the skills and tools just become hacks we try and most likely don't sustain. Instead, I need to identify something that will serve as a compass point, my true north for which I constantly aim.

My *why* is simple: God has given me incredible opportunities to influence others through my training, coaching, and teaching. I want to steward those opportunities by being fully present and *available*. That's it. Not always easy to accomplish in practice, but that's what motivates me. If I keep that larger *why* in mind, and if you do too, it will serve you well in working toward sustainable development.

Second, after, and only after, you've identified your *why*, as I discussed a bit earlier, it's important to identify *how* you will get to where you are going. To do this, work on identifying skills that can help you bridge the gap. My example above focusing on the woman who wanted to move from being "knowledgeable" to "innovative" illustrates this. Before you move on to Chapter 8, take some time to complete the Gap Analysis and reflection questions using those important suggestions below.

Personalize It

Part I: Conduct your own "gap analysis"

"The Leader I am Now is…"	"The Leader I'd Like to Be is…"

Part II: Insights & Action

What's your *WHY*?

Why do you want to get to where you want to go?

How can it help you serve others and be the best version of yourself as a leader?

How will you get to where you want to go?

What skills and/or actions can help you bridge the gap?

What resources can you seek out (e.g., coaching, training) to help you bridge the gap?

SECTION III

Commit to Action

In this section I present three core practices to help you take what you learn from being vulnerable and authentic, as well as reflecting and projecting (Chapters 4-7, Section II) and put them into practice. In other words, do something with all that info you gather and make sure it sticks! I present part 2 of our model of authentic leader development by looking at practicing small, measuring progress, and practicing accountability.

8

Practice Small

M y father-in-law Kevin is an incredible woodworker and builder. Just about anything he thinks up, he can build. I've had the good fortune of witnessing many (and helping with a few) amazing projects over my 14 years of marriage to his daughter, from small bathroom build-outs to basements-turned-wood shops to adding 100 square feet of decking to an already impressive back deck on their home. Side note: my wife picked up a ton of his skills over the years, so our houses have benefitted over the years in the form of countless D.I.Y. projects. You'll hear more about our D.I.Y. projects in the final chapter, so stay tuned…

Of all the projects Kevin has completed, I think his most impressive is one he finished in spring 2024. He built a 150 square foot, rustic log cabin on the side of a mountain in the back of their property in Tennessee. It's a quintessential mountain pad, with no electricity or frills, but with all the touches that give it the perfect feel—from its metal roof to its fire-torched exterior, taking the rustic look to the next level. If you look at it, it just looks like a challenging project. It's on the side of a mountain, for one, not to mention the size of the lumber used in the project.

But arguably the most incredible thing about it is that he built it by hand, by himself. In the story of this cabin lies one of the most valuable pieces of advice I can give you for your leadership development: **think big, but practice small**. My father-in-law had a big dream, a big vision. A cabin in the mountains qualifies, right? But this project was only possible one step, one bolt, one board, one screw—at a time. So it goes with you and with your leadership development. Have big dreams for yourself but start small.

Zeke is a mid-level leader in a Fortune 100 retail company who attended a training seminar I facilitated recently. He was part of a cohort of around 50 leaders nominated to take part in an aspiring leaders program, a semi-annual offering at the company. It's a two-day event, complete with executive speakers, team building, business 101-type talks, and skill builds from facilitators like me.

The topic of the seminar was Professional Presence: Building a Leadership Brand. We spend time working on core communication skills (e.g., listening, connecting with your audience, asking effective questions) in various communication contexts (e.g., one-on-one, leading teams, public speaking). We do a lot in three hours. The leaders have chances to have paired and table-top discussions, do some scripting and free-writing, and share their experiences with me for feedback.

Something always happens throughout the session and at the end. The leaders are challenged to note takeaways and what they intend to do about them (i.e., action). I always give them one key piece of advice: *practice small*. What I'm encouraging them to do is pick one, maybe two, key takeaways and give it some time for intentional practice.

Zeke was an active participant in the session, so I wasn't surprised when, one week later, he emailed me with some questions. In fact, a lot of questions. He had been incorporating the lessons and takeaways he had in the session, along with some core practices, such as the Mental Replay tool (see Chapter 6). He shared with me several examples of recent conversations he's had and some of the practices he's incorporating. Side note: as a facilitator, there's hardly anything more satisfying than hearing about how your trainees are using what they've learned. After seeing one of his completed Mental Replay worksheets and guiding him with some feedback, I simply asked, mostly rhetorically: "Zeke, do you think you're trying to do too much, trying to change too much?" He agreed he was. I replied, "Just remember, practice small."

See, when we learn something, especially if the content is delivered in a compelling way, we tend to want to try stuff out. It's a good instinct. As mentioned, you need to practice what's preached. But **if you want something to stick, practice small**. The payoff then comes when that one thing leads to other things, other actions, other habits.

The key to practicing small is to think about two things: skill and timeline. For the first part, skill, there are two potential starting points. You can start with a skills gap or pain point you know you need to work on. This could be identified from your own Gap Analysis you've performed (Chapter 7), or it could be from something more formal like your performance evaluation. Or your boss might just tell you something you need to work on. Either way, this gives you a concrete skill based on current challenges or experiences. This is arguably the most common starting point. Another starting point is simply to start with the skill rather than a specific pain point. I might notice, for instance, that my colleague is a great listener. Maybe I've never received any negative feedback about my listening, but I know how he listens and how it makes me feel when he listens to me that way and that drives me to be better. Think of the former as a deficit perspective and the latter as an opportunity perspective.

Whatever the starting point, you want to identify the skill and then concrete ways you'll practice the skill. One simple way to identify something concrete is to ask yourself, *"what does success look like when it comes to that skill?"* In other words, if I develop and practice the skill more effectively, what will change, what would be different, what would I do differently? If, for instance, I am wanting to learn to be more assertive because my boss tells me I let people walk over me, I could make a commitment to myself and my accountability partner (more on that in Chapter 10) that I am going to lean into difficult conversations and not shy away from them. Likewise, if you're wanting to be a better listener, your marker of success and concrete practice is to ask more questions rather than give advice.

The next step is to put a timeframe on it. For instance, I am going to make a concerted effort to lean into difficult conversations when they come up for this quarter. Now, this doesn't mean that when this quarter is up you either abandon it altogether and revert to your old ways or that you're an expert at assertiveness or have it figured out. You're just committing to something over a specific period. This will help you avoid doing too much and trying to change too much.

So, if we put it all together, **practicing small is about picking one concrete skill and practicing it over a defined period of time**. Later, I'll show you how you can combine practicing small with accountability for a potent combination.

Picking one thing to work on honors a core component of having success in any endeavor: focus. Gary Keller and Jay Papasan, in their book *The One Thing*, highlight what they call the "focusing question", "*What's the one thing I can do such that by doing it everything else will be easier or unnecessary?*"[28] Asking this one question in the context of goal setting and task management unlocks incredible focus and execution. If we apply this to the context of leader development, then, practicing small helps us focus on one thing that will address what we need most, when we need it. And the compounding effects can be rich. Assertiveness might just help us unlock success in other areas of our lives, making other things easier.

Takeaways & Action Items – The 3-30-90 Method

In Chapter 12, I expand on this more, but according to the 70-20-10 model of learning and development, formal learning (e.g., training, courses, coaching sessions) constitutes a tiny portion of our learning—only about 10%. The rest comes from collaborative relationships (20%) and on-the-job learning through challenging assignments and projects (70%). Here I'll discuss a simple but effective method of making the most out of the connection between the 10% of learning that happens in a classroom or coaching session and the rest of the pie. The key is to note takeaways from your learning and then commit to putting them into practice. But, going a step further, I recommend using the 3-30-90 method of takeaways and action items.

Using **the 3-30-90 method is all about making commitments in loosely defined time frames**. In my experience,

---

[28] Keller, Gary, & Papasan, Jay. *The One Thing: The Surprisingly Simple Truth about Extraordinary Results*. Hachette, 2013.

leaders can have a hard time knowing what to work on, how, and when. This method helps because it's about deciding what you can put into practice in the next 3 days, the next 30 days, and the next 90 days. Or short, medium, and long(er)-term commitments. The benefits are two-fold. The method a) helps you make concrete, defined commitments, and b) ensures you won't bite off more than you can chew. Remember, "think big, practice small" is the goal. Some things need to be tried right away; others require long-term thinking, planning, and practicing. On a practical note, certain contexts where you need to practice might be further down the road.

Chances are if a training was effective, it provided you with concrete, tangible skills and techniques you can try out, as well as mindsets or frameworks you can use. The time-frames don't need to be too precise so don't overthink it. Your 3-day might just be in the next 3-5-7 days. For example, if on a Thursday you learn about public speaking skills, and you know you have a presentation coming up next week, you could commit to using something you learned then.

Here are some examples of how you might apply these three timeframes based on different topics and skills. As you read through these, note that they identify a specific skill or practice and provide a quick "why" or description for each one. Each one starts with a verb, indicating that I plan to do something concrete and specific. The description is important for providing a tag for quick reference and reminding yourself of the impact of the practice—in other words, why it's useful.

3-day

- Practice "intentional" eye contact method weekly briefing next week to build inclusivity with my team.

- Use the "purposeful pausing" technique learned in the training session to help slow me down and create better pace.

- Practice "future-based listening" in my conversation with Cathy next week to help create alignment and buy-in on the change of direction.

30-day

- Incorporate the "Assertion-Evidence Method" of slideshow design during sales presentation in the spring off-site seminar to aid in the persuasiveness of my message.

- Develop my "make it your own" story to use as my intro and hook to help me personalize it and create alignment with my audience.

- Use the "Five Whys" technique in my monthly check-in with Dave to help him look for "points of purpose" in his work and keep him encouraged.

90-day

- Utilize the "Audience 101" worksheet in preparing for my presentation at the fall Summit Series to help me connect with my audience and create alignment between us.

- Incorporate the "Simple Structure" technique for my Toastmasters presentation this summer.

- Conduct a "Mental Replay" after each weekly check-in to give me a large sample size and help me better understand my communication tendencies.

Hopefully with those examples provided, you can begin to see how to incorporate the 3-30-90 framework into your development work, whether it's training or coaching. The combination of starting small to practice small via a 3-day commitment will help you build some of those quick wins that are crucial for success. As a final word of encouragement, and by now it won't surprise you to read this, I recommend sharing these time-bound commitments with others. Hopefully you can see how things come together, but **by adding collaboration via sharing your specific commitments, you will compound the impact of your learning and development.** In the end, I encourage you to think big, dream big, but start by practicing small.

Personalize It

Part I: Dream It

What's your big dream, big vision for yourself? (Refer back to your Gap Analysis from Chapter 7 if that's helpful)

What does success look like—how will you know if you've gotten there?

Part II: Plan It

Think of something you've recently learned or worked on that serves your big vision/dream for yourself. This could be a specific skill or technique you learned or a class you've taken or book you've read. Map out your takeaways and commitments using the 3-30-90 timeframes format.

What can I put into practice to help me get closer to who I want to be?	
3-Days	
30-Days	
90-Days	

9

Measure Progress

The added benefit of practicing small is that it makes **measurement doable**. The smaller and more concrete the skill, the easier it is to measure whether the skill is being practiced, and correctly. Depending on what you're trying to develop, measurement could be relatively straightforward and simple or it can be more challenging.

The distinction between hard and soft skills, for instance, might provide some clarity. Chances are that things you're wanting to develop and get better at will fall into one of those two buckets or be somewhere in the middle. For the record, I'm not a big fan of that hard/soft skill distinction because of the implicit hierarchy those two things can connote—hard skills being more important—but most people get the difference, so stick with me here.

Let's take some examples and create a continuum from the hardest and most concrete to the softest. A helpful exercise right now would be for you to stop and brainstorm a few things you've been working on recently or would like to work on. Then, see where those things would fit on this continuum. On one side, you have a hard, concrete skill such as typing speed. If you currently type at 50 words per minute and you take some classes or read up on how to increase your typing speed, you should expect that within a month or so, depending on how much time you're putting in, that you should improve. It would be easy to measure your progress, for instance, if you set a goal to go from 50 words per minute to 60 to 70 and so on, each month, for three months. Hard skill, simple measurement.

Moving along the continuum, let's say you were working on your time management. Time management is a goal and a process that has many hard and soft elements, so measurement might is already a bit more complicated. There are ways you can use Microsoft Outlook more effectively, use alarms, and so on that will help you (hard skills) and you can learn to be more effective at things like setting boundaries and "tactful refusal," a.k.a., saying no (soft skills).

Let's say you and your team needed to improve your customer service in your call center. You could consider this to be a skill with soft and hard components. After all, dealing with an angry customer has some art and science to it. You have policies and procedures to follow but also must be able to keep your balance when dealing with issues and challenges that arise. What you could do is simply look at hard metrics like customer complaints, callbacks, and time on calls, and track their movement pre- and post-skills training. You would hope that you'd get fewer complaints and callbacks, and it would take less time to solve problems if the training is working.

Next, imagine you're wanting to work on your executive presence, a skillset with many subskills that range from hard to soft. Presence involves *who* you are personally (i.e., your character), *what* you know and your business savvy (i.e., your acumen), as well as *how* you "show up" or communicate (i.e., your delivery). Additionally, presence is a skillset that is handy across just about every domain of leadership, whether you're having a one-on-one meeting and giving feedback, leading your team in a planning session, or standing on stage delivering a speech to 500 people at your annual sales meeting.

Finally, I would argue on the far side, the soft side, of the continuum, would be something like active listening. There are things one can and should "do" that firm it up a bit such as paraphrasing and body language, but so much of active listening is about mindset and perspective, both soft skills. For instance, the mindset and purpose with which you enter a conversation can play a big role in how successful you are at listening on deep levels. It's simply hard to measure how you're developing in those areas. Doable, but difficult.

Next, let's look at some examples in depth via a small case study to help you see how you can take some of these softer skills and measure them effectively. We'll continue with the presence example, as it's a fitting one because of the multitude of skills that comprise it.

Although some of the skills within presence and other skill sets might be soft skills, they no-doubt have hard, concrete results, which are certainly measurable. **The key for you is to define what success looks like as you're working on a given skill.** A bit of an extended example here will help illustrate how you might take something "soft" within presence, or similar, and measure it based on concrete results.

I coached a client a few years back, we'll call him Larry, who was a senior executive in I.T. services for a global financial services firm. Larry had gotten to his role because of his uber sharp technical skills and competence. On the softer side of things, Larry was witty and had a quirky sense of humor. Because he had such specialized knowledge in his field, notably in information security, privacy, and data protection, Larry was called on regularly to deliver briefs and trainings to his team and similar ones in his orbit. Larry quirky sense of humor and lightheartedness served him well as he helped people see the value of his content, especially since most found it dry and "not in their wheelhouse." Let's be honest, you can only do so much to make password protection and two-factor authentication sexy.

But a funny thing happened at the end of his presentations: nothing. No comments, no questions. Larry and his leader who hired me to coach him saw this as a problem and identified presence as a target of some development work for him. Even though we were committing to a six-month partnership, it was important that we identify some markers for success so that we knew what a successful coaching partnership would be. This is nothing magical, by the way; it's the basic definition of what coaching is supposed to do. But stick with me here because I want to show how you can take something you're working on and create some measurability, even if you don't have a coach to help you walk through it.

Early in the partnership, Larry did some mock presentations for me, we talked through his presentation style, as well as the content. I asked Larry what he would like to be different. This is the proverbial question everyone should ask themselves or have it asked, "*What's wrong with the way things are now?*" Larry said, simply, that no one asked questions, and he wanted them to. The second goal of his was that he wanted to get invited to deliver more presentations beyond the handful of teams and divisions that he commonly gets asked to speak to, as well as to the broader parent company. Larry also had a long-term goal of moving up in the company and being head over a much larger division at the parent company.

With these outcomes in mind, then we could work on strategies of presentation engagement that would lead to more questions, more visibility. We worked on storytelling, asking questions to get the audience more involved, and working through examples more slowly. Essentially, beginning with his outcomes in mind gave us actions to practice and focus on. Larry was pleased when, after about two months of intentional practice and honing his skills, he was getting more questions and being asked to speak as an expert more broadly. In short, he had a way to measure his progress, and he was happy with the results.

To recap, the first thing that might help is to take the skill you want to work on and the actions you intend to practice with and determine where it fits on the hard-soft continuum. Hard skills are usually more measurable and have numbers attached to them. Then, decide what your outcomes are—what does success look like, or what would you want to look or sound different as a result? **Even the softest of skills should have some concrete outcomes you can identify**. Once you get to that point, you're able to measure your progress.

I Am...

I'd like to offer another framework to practice measuring your progress. At first, it seems like a soft practice for soft skills, but I find that it has tangible and valuable results that accompany it. I encourage you to create three Leadership "I Am" statements to help you identify who you are and would like to be and, crucially, to help you measure your progress as a leader. The original inspiration behind this practice came from Craig Groeschel, in an episode of "The Craig Groeschel Leadership Podcast." Since I heard him talk about this practice, I have used it with countless leaders, and it remains one of the most valuable tools in my development tool kit.

To start, I'll give you my three I am statements:

- I am a bold leader.

- I am a leader who can be counted on.

- I am a leader who encourages.

I Am is declarative and powerful. It is identity based and projects into the future (see Chapter 7). It doesn't just say "I want to be." Instead, as habits research would show us, it projects into the future by saying who you actually are at your core, even if you are actively working toward being that.[29] Once you say who you are, you are on the hook. You can hold yourself accountable for progress toward that identity and other people can too.

Here are a few words of caution and guidance about crafting your I Am statements. First, when I train leaders on creating I Am statements, I never have this as an in-session activity for one simple reason: you need to take your time when writing them. I recommend taking 3-4 weeks to craft these I Am statements. The statements are aspirational, but they need to be authentic and true to who you are. Therefore, take your time and reflect on your work, your life, your work-flow, the people around you, and perhaps many other factors, as you are thinking about the I Am statements.

---

[29]   Clear, James. *Atomic Habits*.

Notice how you react to situations and do lots of reflection. Some things to consider, observe, and data mine (see Chapter 6):

- What gives you energy?

- What zaps your energy?

- What would you like to do more/less of?

- Where do you find that you can and do make the biggest impact with others?

- Where would you like to do more to make a bigger impact?

- Where are you at your best?

- What are the actions and activities that would help you make an impact?

By taking time to reflect on those types of questions in your environment, you can craft more authentic and realistic I Am statements.

Second, I recommend making the I Am statements short and sweet. They need to lead to concrete actions, so generally speaking, shorter ones will do that. Third, share these I Am statements with others. Ask them for their feedback. Do they see these in you? Where can they offer advice and guidance to you and help you live them out?

The final piece of advice, and this is equally important as the I Am statements themselves, is to create at least one I Will statement as a corollary to each I Am statement. For example, mine are:

- I am a bold leader.
  - Therefore, I Will lean into difficult conversations.
- I am a leader who can be counted on.
  - Therefore, I Will manage my time well so I can be available to everyone.
- I am a leader who encourages.
  - Therefore, I Will give detailed feedback to my students and training clients.

As you read the I Will corollaries, take note that they are phrased in the affirmative rather than the negative. I didn't say "I will not avoid difficult conversations." Instead, phrase them to indicate what you *will* do. Finally, just as you share your I Am statements with others on the front end as you are creating them, I recommend you share the I Am and I Will statements with others for accountability's sake.

As you review your progress as a leader in any of the areas you're working to develop—whether they are "soft" or "hard" skills—**your I Am statements are your true north for your development**. In a given quarter or semester, were you true to your I Am statements? Did you act on your I Will statements? If not, make note of the situations, triggers, people, etc., that made it challenging and caused you to slip. Give yourself some grace because, after all, you are human. Remember, the goal is progress, not perfection. As James Clear says in *Atomic Habits*, each positive behavior (habit) is like a vote for the person you want to be. You can still win an election without getting all the votes. You just want most of the votes going in the right direction! Additionally, The I Am and I Will statements give you something for your intentionality–something to consciously bring your attention to (see Chapter 3), and measure progress against. As a bonus, you can also use the I Am statements as a cross-reference checkpoint with other techniques in this book. For example, you can conduct a Mental Replay about a meeting you just led and assess whether you were true to who you are, according to your I Am statement/s. Likewise, you might use an I Am statement as a point to work toward that you identify on your Gap Analysis. The possibilities are endless!

Measuring your development as a leader is tricky business. Indeed, many leadership development practitioners (e.g., trainers, coaches) shy away from talks of return on investment (ROI) precisely because development is hard to measure, particularly when one is developing "soft" skills. Nevertheless, identifying specific indicators of success (i.e., "what does success look like?"), as the examples in this chapter illustrate, can give you the best chance of measuring your progress. Furthermore, your I Am statements are your litmus test. They are your personal accountability tool to help you live up to—*measure* up to—who you want to be. And the bonus is that when something's measurable, it makes it easier to share it with others and foster a culture of accountability. We turn there next.

Personalize It

If you were to map out a skill on the soft-to-hard continuum, where would it fall?

A soft skill I want to develop is

The "hard", tangible behaviors that make up this soft skill are:

My three leadership I Am statements are

1. _____
2. _____
3. _____

Based on those I AM Statements,

1. I Will _____
2. I Will _____
3. I Will _____

10

Practice Accountability

A 2022 study found that 75% of people said they would be more likely to go to the gym more routinely and work on their health if they just had more of one thing. Any guesses what it was? I've asked this question to thousands of leaders and the most common response I get is "time." The next most common is "money." Truth is, we would all love more time and more money, right? But the answer? 75% said they just need someone to go with them.[30]

As it turns out, social influence (a.k.a. peer pressure), which starts when we're kids, matters in all domains of life. **What's true in working out is true in working on yourself—accountability matters.** Just a heads up, this is one of

---

[30]   Mema, Ensela et al. "Social Influences on Physical Activity for Establishing Criteria Leading to Exercise Persistence. *PLoS ONE*, 2022.

the longest chapters in this book, and that's no accident. In my experience, although it's absolutely vital, accountability is one of the most under-utilized components of leader development. Leader, I implore you—don't make this mistake! When it comes to your development, don't do it without much reflection, and don't go at it alone.

But *how* you practice accountability makes a big difference. I encourage two forms: self and other accountability. You need a simple, doable way to keep track of your progress personally, and you need to bring someone along with you on the journey.

Self-Accountability

A tried-and-true method of self-accountability is a daily reflection/journaling practice. In my experience there is a tendency to overthink this or try to get a bit too fancy. I always tell my clients the best system is one you will actually use. Some like to type their reflections, others like to write. Personally, I keep it old school, and opt for a 5x7, ruled, hardback notebook. At any given time, I might have three or four notebooks going. For instance, at the time of this writing, I have four notebooks in rotation. First, a daily spiritual journal where I record takeaways from my morning prayer and Bible reading time. Currently I'm on a teaching sabbatical, so I have a sabbatical reflection journal where I record daily thoughts, tasks I complete, and general goings on. My third notebook is book ideas, many of which you'll encounter in these pages, of course. Finally, I have a "dream" notebook, where I simply record business ideas.

The question that gives people pause on journaling is, *what do I write?* You could make the argument that what you record in your notebooks is important, but I believe the most important thing is whether you record. Some days I record what I think are profound insights; other days I literally just describe what happened that day the way a court reporter would. To give you an example, here's an entry, verbatim, from my sabbatical notebook yesterday.

2/7/24 – Wednesday

- Prayer and devotional – Things that aren't in God's will will eventually turn to ashes.

- Client workshop 9a-12p went well. 4 on the call but they were great – lots of great takeaways!

- Errands with B – love this time we have together!

- Music with Emma – proud of her hard work.

- Family time watching old family movies – good times!

Take a minute to look over the entry. What do you notice? If you wrote this, what might you glean from it? How could it help you? In full transparency, I haven't analyzed it myself at this point in my writing, but if I had, here's what I could pick up on. The takeaway from the devotional time is self-evident to me; I want to be in the center of God's will for my life. I can reflect on the workshop and remember the 4 participants on the call and my approach to them and the content. Specifically, I believe my use of dialogue and lots of questions helped them provide more takeaways. I can remember to always be intentional with those techniques, especially on that topic. Points three, four, and five about my wife, daughter, and our family, respectively, are simply just gratitude, always fitting entries for a journal. And they're reminders about my priorities. They also remind me that there's just no better way to end the day than with quality family time.

So, now, take a few minutes again to consider what you could glean if these were your entries. I know when I started journaling it was hard to know what to write, so hopefully these examples provide that bump you need to just get started.

In the previous two chapters, we discussed practicing small and measuring your progress. Your journal is the place where those two things come together. As you practice, record how you're doing—good and bad—and that gives you a form of introspection helpful for measurement.

A tool that I include in the online toolkit for you to use is a Brand Development Tracker.[31] I developed this tool for a recent client partnership. This business wanted to provide their people with resources to help leaders develop their leadership "brand" and measure their progress. The tool itself includes guidelines and instructions on how to complete it, so I won't spend time unpacking it here. For now, just know that your leadership "brand" is a combination of who you've been in the past and where you'd like to go. And self-accountability and reflection is vital to knowing those answers. It brings together many of the things you've been reading about. **Tracking the development of your "brand" is not only personal, but it also invites others into the process.**

Other Accountability

Remember the other piece of advice I started this chapter with—don't go at it alone. I repeat a phrase cited in a

---

[31]   www.authenticleaderdevelopment.com/resources/toolkit

previous chapter: "Despite our common cultural notion of 'self'improvement, the most successful efforts to self-improve have other people at their core."[32]

Other accountability is a crucial part of leader development for many reasons, but simply put, **leadership happens in the context of other people, so it stands to reason that leadership development should as well**, right? I often share a truism with my clients to help them see the value in other accountability. Chances are, the people around you, the people you lead, know your deficiencies and what you need to work on anyway, so why not share with them and let them help hold you accountable? I joke with them that if you go to one of your colleagues or direct reports and say, "hey, I really need to work on my listening skills, so can you help hold me accountable for that?", chances are they will be thinking, "yes, you really do need to work on that." Depending on your relationship, they might tell you that and you might both get a little laugh out of it. When I use this example in workshops, it gets a chuckle every time, mostly because people realize how true it is.

Recently I partnered with a large, global business to offer a series on "time management," which I refer to as "focus and attention management." The business provides a variety of services including cybersecurity, risk assessment, I.T. monitoring, and customer support programs. The team I was training was senior account executives from across one state who are responsible for large, high-impact accounts. These are busy folks with high demands on their time and attention. The structure of the three-part series was, first, a 30-minute kick-off session to introduce the tools and a critical "Time Audit" they would be asked to complete over the course of three

---

[32] *Rely on Others to Improve Yourself.* Harvard Business Review, 2017.

weeks (see Henry Cloud's work for more information on time auditing[33]). Second, a 90-minute session four weeks later to review their Time Audit results and introduce core tools and practices. Finally, we held a 90-minute session six weeks later to review their calendars, check their progress, and offer final tips and techniques. A key part of the time between session two and three was their finding an accountability buddy to share their calendars with and do check-ins periodically.

One leader, we'll call him Denny, shared his experience with his "time management buddy." Denny created a template that served as a framework for his work and life activities. The template was a relatively simple Excel spreadsheet, mirroring his calendar, that he would use to intentionally plan out his day, ensuring that he could carve out the time he needed to prioritize most effectively. Importantly, he structured the template to fit his normal travel pattern (in the car a lot) and other structural components of his normal routine.

For Denny, creating the template was a game changer because it was his way of "practicing small," but most importantly because it was a simple tool he could then share with his buddy. The two of them connected and Denny's template offered a format that his buddy and others in the cohort could mirror.

One question I get often is, "whom should be my accountability partner?" or "who would make a good mentor?" These are great questions, and chances are you have thought them as well, perhaps now. A quick note: not to get too caught up on terminology, but a lot of people ask about mentorship versus accountability. A full dive into that is beyond our scope here, so in this context, an accountability partner might be more of a short-term connection for the

---

[33]   "Time and Energy Audit." www.boundaries.me/audit.

purposes of working on a specific skill or skillset (e.g., professional presence, time management). A mentor might be more long-term and someone you invite into your journey as you look to develop and work on yourself across multiple areas.

Whichever term you like, **I suggest looking at accountability partners or mentors at three levels—someone below your level, someone at your level, someone above your level**. Next, I talk about "candidates" at each level and provide you with a toolkit of questions you can use to guide some of your accountability questions. You'll see some overlap on questions you can ask, but the diversity in responses, of course, comes in the diversity of the levels of accountability partners.

First, when I say "below" your level, this could be age or position. For instance, for years I've had an accountability partner and mentor who was, at one point, my student. We'll call him Manny. In this case, we're basically talking about what is commonly referred to as "reverse mentoring." When Manny was in school, he interned for me for my training and consulting business, Jeremy Fyke Leader Development. Although Manny is half my age, he possesses wisdom well beyond his years. Add to that the fact that he and I are aligned in our faith, so he made for a great accountability partner as I was growing my business, dealing with those stressors, and continually working on being who I need to be to represent Christ to everyone I come across. When Manny was my intern, he contributed in ways that were more strategic than tactical, opposite of what we sometimes experience with interns. It was a fitting accountability relationship because Manny pushed me and challenged me on blind spots and areas of opportunity and growth.

In my experience, people younger than you are excellent accountability partners because they just see things from different points of view. What you think are big deals, they might not, and vice-versa. They can give you fresh takes and fresh enthusiasm you might just need to handle the challenges you face. As a bonus, it allows you to pour into them, even though you might be seeking out *their* help. After all, mutual accountability is the best path to a successful relationship in which you both grow.[34]

So, how young should an ideal accountability partner be? Certainly, age is an easy factor, so you could arbitrarily say 20 years, for example. But rather than only thinking of age, think of stage or season. For instance, at the time when we met, Manny was 20 and I was 39. Yes, we had a couple of decades between us, but he was two to three stages or seasons behind me in life. He was in college, which simultaneously feels like forever ago and just yesterday. Know what I mean? But objectively speaking, it was definitely a few stages of life ago—before kids, before marriage, before a chocolate Goldendoodle, mortgage, life insurance, and so on. So, my advice here is to be sure to pick someone at least a couple of stages behind you. You might be 30 and have an accountability partner who's 20 but clearly in a different season.

One place to look for younger accountability partners is to plug into a local university. Universities are always looking for leaders and business partners in their communities. If you need a place to start, connect with me and I'll help you get started. All universities have some version of a career and professional development team, so that is also a good place to start. Chances are, there will be opportunities to connect

---

[34] H.H. Kelley and J.W. Thibaut, *Interpersonal Relations: A Theory of Interdependence.* 1978.

for job fairs, guest lectures, and convocation events on campus. Get creative with it and keep an open mind.

If it's not someone younger, someone new to their job or role can be a great accountability partner. Look for those in your organization who are starting out and see if you can serve as accountability partners. If your organization doesn't have a former mentoring/accountability system, it's time to create one.

Someone new to their job or role is a great accountability partner for one critical reason. As they are starting out in their jobs, they might not have a lot of experience being led, so they can share their preferences, likes and dislikes, and what makes them tick. As you're working on your authenticity, vulnerability, and reflection, they are your sounding board. As you practice small and try to measure your progress, they share their perspective on how you're doing. As a bonus, you serve an important role in helping them get a dose of reality as they enter the workforce. Indeed, they might have preferences that simply aren't realistic, especially depending on what field they're going into. As an educator, I've seen my share of idealistic students sharing their hopes and dreams for the workplace, only to have them brought down to reality, many times in a healthy way once they begin their careers. Again, there's great opportunity for mutual accountability and mentorship there.

Questions for "below you" accountability partners:

- How do you see _____ (win, challenge, issue, problem)?

- What would you do if you were me?

- How would you handle _____ (win, challenge, issue, problem)?

- What's the toughest challenge you've recently faced?
  - How did you handle that challenge?
- What should my next step be in dealing with _____ (win, challenge, issue, problem)?

Your next accountability partner is someone at or near your level, again either age or position. For obvious reasons, someone around your age most likely is in a similar season as you and therefore, can relate to what you're trying to handle and the challenges you face. For instance, at the time of this writing, I'm 44 and my two kids are 7 and 10. I have a friend of mine who is a pastor, 46-years-old, with three kids. Granted, he has one more kid than me, which of course is significant, but we're close in our ages and stages of life. Importantly, he and I are similarly aligned on our focus areas for our leadership. A couple of years back I led his leadership team through trainings and exercises around effective communication and teamwork. Throughout the planning and in the follow-up process, he and I shared wins and challenges, struggles and setbacks. He's someone I look to as a mentor and accountability partner.

A good candidate for a near-your-level accountability partner might be similar to the proximity of mine. People tend to flock together, so chances are you have plenty you can choose from, age-wise. Your accountability partner might also be someone in your orbit at work at a similar level. Perhaps you interact often on projects or in meetings. You might even depend on each other for each of your respective successes. **Interdependence creates many opportunities for accountability**, whether we're intentional about it or not. If that is true, and I believe it is, let's be intentional about it—about challenging each other, about sharpening each other.

At work, since someone at your level is most likely experiencing similar things as you, you can share wins, challenges, and struggles. I encourage you to be more vulnerable with this accountability partner because the level of relatability should be higher. You'll have more in common and be going through similar things, so there should be more opportunities for openness and honesty.

Questions for your "near you" accountability partner:

- How do you see _____ (win, challenge, issue, problem)?

- How would you handle _____ (win, challenge, issue, problem)?

- What would you do if you were me?

- What's your biggest growth area in your leadership currently?

- I'm really trying to get better at _____ (insert development/skill area, e.g., listening). What are your successes and setbacks with that?

- What advice do you have for me in trying to get better at _____ (development/skill area)?

- You seem to be really good at _____ (development/skill area). How have you been successful in that area?

Your final accountability partner is someone, shall we say, more seasoned than you. It might be someone older and/or with more experience. This person might be someone at your company that you look up to because he or she has influenced you, or it might be someone outside of work. Perhaps you admire their focus and determination or their track record of success. Chances are, it's probably a combination. It might be a friend or a friend's parent you've known for a long time.

So, how old should this accountability partner be? Where should he/she be in his/her career? Similar to my words earlier about your "below you" accountability partner, age can be a decent metric to consider, but also arbitrary. For instance, you could pick someone 20 years older than you, but I recommend thinking about stages and/or seasons again.

My "above me" accountability partner is and has been for some time, my father. At this writing, I'm 44, my father is 74. He has 30 years on me, but he's also retired after a long, successful career in sales, marketing, and business development. He retired as senior vice president of a consumer goods packaging company. He also serves as an elder at his church, leads multiple teams, trains people, and is an informal mentor to so many. Basically, he has lots of wisdom to go around. He's at a different life stage and season, so he's a fitting partner for me. He helps keep me accountable in many areas of development—spiritual, relational, and business. We do Bible readings and devotionals together. Occasionally, we preach at churches, him more than me. When we do, we share our notes, thoughts, and outlines.

A few years back I co-founded Two Heads Hot Sauce, a company my buddy and I started just for fun out of his kitchen. Our hobby and passion project turned into a booming business within about six months. We sold nearly 10,000 bottles in our first year in business. We weren't on track to get rich and retire or anything from it, but it was a bonafide business that required serious and steady leadership. It required leadership and leadership skills that I wasn't sure I possessed, frankly. From budgeting to visioning to decision making to having difficult conversations, it was the most challenging thing I had ever done. It was awesome, it was fun, *and* it was hard. My father was my sounding board for just about everything.

See, my business partner is an absolute genius in the kitchen. Everything we made and sold as a business came from his brain, off the top of his head. He just thinks of how flavors might come together and voila—deliciousness. And, for 95% of what we made, it worked. But he just wasn't as interested in the business side of it. That was my domain, my interest, and my expertise. But I needed help. If you've ever been new to a role, new to a project, or new to a business, you know what I'm talking about. After all, part of being an effective leader is knowing what you don't know (see Chapter 4 on vulnerability).

As I was growing and groaning my way through leading the business, I was needing to bounce so many things off my father. And I had another incredible resource— my build-anything father-in-law, whom I introduced in Chapter 8. My father-in-law is a seasoned businessman. A CPA turned full-time pastor and now executive director at a large nonprofit, the dude has some serious chops. He provided an incredible service for us by managing our books for nearly two years. He provided not only concrete help with our accounting but advice on the ever-critical corporate/strategy/accounting connection. The truth is, sales and accounting, for instance, don't always like each other or want to speak to each other. Sales wants to just…sell. But accounting knows what and how stuff impacts the bottom line. My father-in-law kept us from wandering off in the woods alone, making silly decisions that he knew would impact us and drive him absolutely crazy when it got downstream to him. We had lots of heart-to-hearts, and in those conversations, I valued his leadership advice as much as his business advice. Not that they're really different, but I digress…

In the end, both of those men came back to help tremendously when, in late 2023 we were able to start the process of selling the business, which we completed in early 2024. My partner and I created something that made money, someone bought it, and it lives on. Win-win. I simply couldn't have done it without the accountability partners in my life.

What can I say? Between my two fathers in my life, I just have some serious muscle in my corner. And you know what? **You have a lot of muscle in your corner, too**. Maybe it's inside your family, maybe it's outside. Find people who are in a different life stage or season than you. Lean into their advice. And as a bonus, you get to be their "below you" accountability partner.

Questions for your "above you" accountability partner:

- How do you see _____ (win, challenge, issue, problem)?

- How would you handle _____ (win, challenge, issue, problem)?

- You seem to be really good at _____ (development/skill area). How have you been successful in that area?

- What's been your biggest leadership lesson in your career?

- How do you describe your leadership style?

- What are examples of some of your leadership wins and challenges?

A few final thoughts on accountability partners. First, don't overthink the age/stage thing and therefore miss the spirit of the arrangement. You might be thinking, I'm 20, should my "below me" partner be 5 or 10 years old? Yes, maybe so! There's an old brainstorming technique where one of the prompts you ask when trying to be innovative is, "What would kindergarteners do?" I've used this in the past and it works wonders. I used it with a group of senior leaders at a big company once and it was amazing. It's funny, entertaining, and it works. Someone 5 or 10 might just give you a wild idea you can build on and a vantage point from which to view your situation. At the very least, someone super young might ask you lots of questions, which might generate some insights. Remember earlier when we talked about the 40,000 questions kids ask by the age of 5? You're bound to get some insight from that tendency to question.

If you're reading this and you're near the end of your career, you might wonder if you can find someone "above you" to serve as your accountability partner. Let's say you're 65 and still love what you do and plan to keep working, so is your accountability partner supposed to be 80 or 85? Why not? Just like I mentioned in the previous paragraph, don't overthink this too much. The point is someone at a different age or stage. If you're still working and want to keep working and know someone who's 75 but retired, that's probably a good accountability partner candidate.

Lastly, there are three prerequisites for an effective accountability partner. These are more important than age and stage. **All accountability relationships must be marked by respect, trust, and seriousness.**

First, your relationship must be marked by mutual respect. You respect them, they respect you. If it's someone that is wildly successful, but you don't respect them, perhaps because of a lack of integrity or humility, it just won't work, at least long term. And chances are you're going to learn some things you don't want to end up emulating anyway, so keep looking. They likewise need to respect you, your journey, your starting point.

Second, your relationship must be marked by trust. This flows from respect, or is rooted in respect, but when there's trust, you'll get honest feedback. Without feedback—honest, tactful, behavior-based feedback—accountability just can't happen. Think about it. You know this to be true in your personal relationships, so why would it be any different here as you're working on your leadership?

Finally, your relationship must be marked by seriousness. I don't mean that you can't have fun and enjoy each other and the process; you can, and you should. What I mean though is that you're both committed and intentional with each other's time and development goals. The first thing I ask when someone asks me to be their accountability partner or mentor, is, *what does that mean to you and what do you need from me in this relationship?* I'm trying to set a tone that I'll take this seriously, so I want them to think about it on the front end. Serious accountability partners keep commitments, push each other when it's warranted, and take deep care of each other's development. They make a personal investment in another person.

Taken together, self and other accountability provide the potent one-two punch you need to be successful. If you can get in the habit of tracking your development with vulnerability and authenticity *and* bring others into that journey, you are well on your way to sustained, authentic development.

Personalize It

Part I: Self & Other Accountability Practice

Spend time journaling throughout the next three days. Write 1 insight/takeaway each day below:

Day 1 _____

Day 2 _____

Day 3 _____

Who can you invite to be your accountability partners at the different levels identified in the chapter?

Below me _____

Near me _____

Above me _____

Part II: Brand Development Tracker

Download and complete the Brand Development Tracker from the online toolkit.
(www.authenticleaderdevelopment.com/resources/toolkit)

Part III: Insights & Action

How will you use the results from your Brand Development Tracker to move you forward?

How will you encourage your accountability partner/s in their journey?

SECTION IV

Openness & Action: The Keys for Authentic Leader Development

This section, which contains one chapter, Chapter 11, brings the previous seven chapters together to present a 2x2 Model of Authentic Leader Development. In Chapters 4-10 we explored how to be open to development and commit to action. Now, I bring all those practices together to explain how you can use the Model for sustained growth and progress toward becoming the leader you were created to be.

11

A Model of Authentic Leader Development: Four Profiles of Authentic Leader Development

The perspective, attitude, and mindset you start with in any endeavor in life make a big difference in future success. With your leader development, you'll need to be prepared and intentional right from the outset to get the most from your efforts. After all, developing your leadership skills and competencies is hard work, so you might as well get it right.

The previous two sections have outlined various practices necessary for sustained development. All those practices coalesce around two crucial factors in authentic leader development: openness and action. Let's first briefly recap the previous seven chapters. To be *open* to development is to be authentic and vulnerable, reflect often, and project the future leader you want to be. But openness is only part of the equation. Of course, you'll then have to *act* on what you learn. To act on what you learn, you'll need to practice small, measure your progress, and be accountable to yourself and others.

In this chapter, I bring all these practices together to present a 2x2, 4-part model for leader development. My goal in developing this model is two-fold. First, you can use it to help you diagnose where you are currently or have been in your development. In other words, this is your starting point. If we were looking at a map, it would say "you are here." And I want to encourage you to give yourself some grace. If your starting point is 0, that is, you are early on in your intentional development, the important thing is that you're starting. My second goal for you is for you to use it as motivation to be intentional about where you want to go. Thus, **the model helps you reflect on the past/present and project into the future (see Chapters 6 & 7).**

If we consider the two factors—openness and action— you can either be low or high on each. Let's explore both factors briefly to set the stage for the chapter. First, you can lack openness or be closed off, not willing to reflect or be honest about your need for development, or you can be highly reflective and vulnerable about your weaknesses. Similarly, just to put this on the ground level more, you can attend a training seminar or workshop, perhaps because you think the topic or facilitator might be interesting or because you feel compelled to go (after all, social pressure is a factor in learning, just like it's a factor in going to the gym, as discussed in the previous chapter). However, if you do not feel personally invested in the content or intentional about it, it is highly unlikely you will experience sustained, meaningful change. On the other hand, if you have or create a personal investment in the topic, for instance, by connecting it to a personal value or deep reason to change, you are more likely to learn on a deeper level and then put that learning into practice. In this case, your openness to development is much higher.

Regarding action, you can be unwilling to do anything about what you know you need to work on, or highly active in working on yourself, trying things out and so on. On a more granular level, you might commit to trying out small actions, "hacks," without sustaining those actions over a meaningful period. You can also try a bunch of new things out without much reflection about how things are going for you, whether they contribute to the identity as a leader you want to be, and so on. Put simply, when you consider openness and action, where you fall on each of these dimensions—low or high—will play an outsized role in your development and the success thereof.

A few quick words as caveats or disclaimers before we dig in. First, what follows is a 2x2 framework, a 4-part model. It's important to point out that human beings are not so simple as to neatly fit into any particular box. The four parts of the model are meant to be descriptive and diagnostic, not necessarily predictive. In other words, I hope by focusing complex things down into four profiles, four sets of behaviors, four parts, it just gives you a starting point to better understand yourself and others. The four parts include mindsets, predispositions, and behaviors, thereby giving you many things to use for reflection and honest appraisal.

These four are also not mutually exclusive, so consider the lines between the four parts to be highly perforated or blurred—your openness and action orientation can change rapidly for a variety of reasons. Thus, like us as individuals, the profiles are also not stable and can be highly subject to time and interest. Indeed, you might find yourself highly open to learning and growing at certain times and seasons and for certain topics. At other times, you're barely keeping your head above water on your tasks and projects, let alone think about things like your leadership development. In short, people are messy, and so are the models and methods that try to understand them.

Exhibit: Model of Authentic Leader Development

Model of Authentic Leader Development

Below, I explain the four parts of the model into different profiles of leader development. The profiles are meant to bring the parts of the model to life, to personify them. The goal here is to help you reflect and really "see" them. I also give each one a brief label meant to describe what someone might look like if they're experiencing, for example, low openness, low action (e.g., "detached"). Crucially, **as you**

read what each might look, sound like, and be caused by, I challenge you to let them read you. As always, do so with candor and vulnerability. Here are some reflection questions to guide you as you read:

- Do you recognize yourself in any of these?

- Do you recognize those you lead in any of these?

- What caused you to have those reactions (e.g., apathy, frenzy)?

- What impact did those reactions have on your development? On your career?

Finally, at the end of each profile, I'll offer advice for how you might help someone who is presenting negative behaviors in the respective profiles. As you read the advice, recognize that it might apply to you as well. In other words, you can turn each piece of advice for helping someone else into a step you can try or ask for help from someone you trust (e.g., an accountability partner).

Oblivious Apathy: Closed Off, Unwilling to Act ("The Detached")

Several years ago, I was blessed to get to work with a large, multinational company on a year-long leader development program. For a leader developer like me, it was a dream program. It was multisession and cohort based, with all the trimmings: accountability groups, manager follow-up in between sessions, and one-on-one and group coaching. But you know the old saying—you can bring a horse to water, but you can't make it drink.

Despite having everything a leader (and a trainer) could want and need, early in the program I noticed a gentleman, about mid-50s seated in the back, leaned back in his chair with his arms folded. If you have spoken to groups with any regularity, it's a look you don't want to see. It communicates, *I can't imagine being less interested in being here.* I speak to groups a lot, so I've learned not to think too much of people's reactions and, for the most part, to ignore the naysayers. But after working with this individual for months and seeing his look—arms folded—repeated numerous times, I have come to learn that he's the prototype for someone who is not open to being developed and unwilling to act on anything he learns. Yes, **he was in the room, but he was not fully there.** The technical term is "presenteeism"– there in body, not in mind. Normally presenteeism refers to an employee who is at work but can't perform because of an illness or other condition. In a leadership development space, their own mindset, attitude, and predispositions are their biggest enemy. If you administer a pre-workshop or pre-program survey where you ask people why they are enrolled in the program, people like this will write, "my boss nominated me," or even less encouraging, "my boss asked me to take part."

What else might we see from someone in this profile? They might have gotten similar feedback about what to work on each quarter, whether formally or informally. Consequently, they might be stuck in their career. If you've been here before, you might be facing common "career derailers." At the top of the list of such derailers, according to workplace competency authority Korn Ferry, are lack of awareness and rigidity.[35] You can't accurately see yourself as others do (i.e., lack of authenticity), and you overestimate

---

[35]   Korn Ferry Advance. "The 12 Most Common Career Derailers." 2020.

your strengths and underestimate your weaknesses. Furthermore, you resist change and struggle outside your comfort zone. Side note: number four on the "career derailers" list is arrogance. Arrogant people are detached, the antithesis of authentic leadership. If you've been here before, chances are you have struggled to get ahead and push past your ceiling as a leader. You might have tremendous business acumen and are highly competent, but your lack of authenticity and unwillingness to change and grow has held you back.

On the other hand, and with a touch of grace, it's worth noting that people here might not know what they don't know. Hence, they are apathetic *and* oblivious. If this has been you, or is someone you lead, the pressure to perform and go-go-go might not leave you/them with the time to be open, let alone to act. If you're leading someone who fits into this part of the model, it's important to help them see clearly. Start with well-portioned developmental feedback that focuses on concrete, small actions. More on how to develop others in Chapter 12.

In the meantime, **another culprit in getting to a point of Oblivious Apathy could be an overemphasis on knowing at the expense of questioning**. In Chapter 4 I discussed how our culture values achievement and execution. Both of those are great and necessary things, but we must learn to live in the tension between knowing and asking. Asking good questions, especially about ourselves, our leadership, and our development, can only make us stronger, at the very least in the medium and long term. Additionally, if you are not open to development and not willing to act, you might not let your feelings speak. Again, in Chapter 4, we looked at how feelings are helpful starting points that cause us to think deeply and ultimately change behavior. In the context of leader development, our feelings are a helpful guide, giving us valuable data points to mine for insights (see Chapter 6).

Finally, if you or someone you know fits into this "box," it might be because of a lack of honest reflection on your past—the good and bad. In Chapter 5, you read about how positive and negative "triggers" are instrumental in our growth and development. Authentically reflecting on those growth points, even the painful negative ones, can be invaluable for helping us move from stuck and apathetic to more productive mindsets and behaviors toward development.

To help someone demonstrating Oblivious Apathy,

- Provide them with concrete examples and evidence for the need to grow and improve (e.g., through performance feedback).

- Offer them specific feedback based on personal experiences and contact with them and their work (e.g., "what I've seen from you is _____").

- Seek first to understand their perspective and experiences with growth and development (negative and positive).

- Help them see/remember areas where they have grown over their lives and careers.

- Set realistic expectations for their progress based on incremental movement toward growth and changes.

- Help them brainstorm positive outcomes from incremental improvements.

- Help them brainstorm "quick wins" they will begin to see from making incremental improvements.

- Partner them with role models to help with growth and development (e.g., match them with someone who fits the "Authentic Development" profile).

Willful Stubbornness: Open to Development, Unwilling to Act ("The Mule")

Sheila was a people leader whom I had the privilege of working with for several months through some training and coaching. She had been in her role for about two years but had been with the company for about five. In the past eight months, she had been given increased responsibilities, due mainly to some restructuring that placed four people beneath her. Sheila took notes on everything she learned and just couldn't get enough content and reading to add to her library. She would often tell me, "I'm a sponge, so keep it coming." You know the problem with sponges? They get wrung out.

So it goes with people who are open to development but fail to put things into action. They simply don't practice what they learn. For the record, Sheila and I worked together to ensure she was not only eager to learn but equally eager to practice; that's what makes all the difference. **They absorb, but there's very little intentionality with what might come out, what might come from that learning.** As with the first profile, Oblivious Apathy, several factors contribute to this fact. At best, people who demonstrate Willful Stubbornness oftentimes learn a lot but don't see concrete or even applicable ways to put things into practice. At worst, and most likely, they might see applicability but don't prioritize action.

They might reflect and learn but don't see how what they are learning applies to them generally or at a specific point in their leadership journey. You might say they are stubborn, stubborn as a Mule. Likewise, they might also just be swamped so they don't have (or make) the time to put things into practice. You'll notice that there is a similarity there between Willful Stubbornness and Oblivious Apathy–being committed to action is low due to the demands of work. Similar result, but for different reasons. Importantly, even though someone in the Willful Stubbornness category might not be putting things into action, the openness to development provides the fertile ground necessary for seeds of development to grow.

Like the previous profile, high openness, low action people can get similar feedback time and again from superiors and peers about things they need to work on. The reason might be obvious, but it's because although they are learning, they are not practicing, not making many changes, if any. Being in this space is tricky because, as a leader of someone who demonstrates this profile, it appears that the information is getting through, but you're not seeing much fruit in terms of change, growth, and development. Likewise, if you are living out this profile, you feel like you are learning, but you are not seeing much fruit from that knowledge.

The key to breaking free from the negative patterns that can result from this profile is moving from information to motivation to transformation. That is, it's the crucial move from information or content that is interesting to you, seeing how it can help, and then actually putting things into practice. For example, if you are learning how to use things such as the Mental Replay or Pause Points (see Chapter 6), the results from those give you information or data to use to change your practices and leadership. However, if you fail to see what to do with that information, or don't make the time to try different things out, it remains just that—information. Likewise, you can read until the end of time about vulnerability and using emotion to help guide you to action, but until you put what you learn into practice, it stays in the realm of information.

Consequently, people who fit the Willful Stubbornness profile often suffer from information overload. They read and absorb a lot, which can be detrimental to your actual growth and development. It acts as a trick because you feel like you are learning but, if you aren't careful, all you are really doing is gathering more information. For example, have you ever read a "good" book but then when someone asks you what it's about or what your takeaways are, you struggle to articulate it? If so, you might be stuck in information and haven't made the shift to action, to transformation.

The final outcome worth noting here is that **people in the Willful Stubbornness profile often see development as a solo enterprise.** In other words, they don't practice "other" accountability, and they might not even practice self-accountability (Chapter 10). See, as they read, study, and take in all that information and content, they tend to keep it to themselves. At best, they journal about what they learn. At worst, they don't do that and they don't share what they are learning with each other. The benefit of putting things into practice is that it makes what you are learning visible—it's out in the open for others to see and offer you feedback.

To help someone demonstrating Willful Stubbornness,

- Seek first to understand their perspective and experiences with growth and development (negative and positive).

- Make sure they can see how to implement interesting content and ideas they have learned, been trained on, read about, etc.

- Help them see how to take a first step toward application.

- Offer safe ways to test out new behaviors or practice techniques learned (e.g., after a leadership development journey).

- Offer your continuous support and encouragement to safely test and receive feedback on new behaviors.

- Help them process performance feedback and translate results into action.

- Help them assess and evaluate new actions compared to previous actions (e.g., assess, "how did they grow and improve?").

- Ensure they practice self-accountability (e.g., through journaling).

- Partner them with an accountability partner to drive learning.

- Model effective accountability practices by sharing your experiences with journaling and meeting with your accountability partner/s.

Shallow Frenzy: Willing to Act, Unclear about Areas for Development ("The Imposter")

James is a leader I met at a workshop I led for a large US-based company in the retail space. He was part of a multi-session, high-potential leadership program. I connected with James right away during the session as well as after. I could tell he was excited, and being relatively new to his leadership role, he was ready to try things out. A lot of things. The danger I anticipated with James is that he was wanting to do something, fix anything, without taking the time to slow down, reflect, and ensure that what he was learning fits with who he is and who he wants and needs to be.

Leaders who fit the Shallow Frenzy profile share similarities with the folks in the Willful Stubbornness category. Specifically, **they can suffer from overload, but instead of information overload, it's just action overload or action frenzy**. It's a "grab and go" approach to learning and development. To be clear, I'm not suggesting it's bad to try out new techniques. Instead, my plea, and this is what I mean by "openness" in the model, is that leaders practice vulnerability, authenticity, and reflection *as* they are trying out new things.

Like the other shortcomings depicted in the previous profiles, leaders arrive at and display Shallow Frenzy for a variety of reasons. For one, the pace of business and therefore the pace of learning drives us to "grab and go" what we can and hurry up and apply it to our work. Instead of taking our time going through the check-out line, aided by someone else, we use self-checkout or the scan-and-go option. Outside of the grocery store metaphors, "just-in-time" training feeds our expectations of being able to learn something quickly and immediately apply it to current opportunities and challenges.

Another factor that isn't necessarily inside your control as a leader and learner is that training offerings tend to pack a lot of content in at the expense of slow down and reflection. They are packed with models, frameworks, theories, and tools, all of which give you steps to try, practices to work on. **Without slow down and reflection (i.e., openness) they can amount to little more than "hacks."** Over time, these hacks cause us to show up as an Imposter because they're not authentic to who we are and who we are becoming.

Shallow Frenzy oftentimes takes the form of trying out leadership hacks, bolstered by what look like quick wins and resolutions to deep, challenging problems. For example, if you are wanting to learn to delegate better, yes, you can learn a 4-step method for better delegation. But if you don't do the deep identity work of getting to the root of why you struggle to delegate in the first place, I submit to you that your application of the 4-step method will not sustain long term, if even medium term. Robert Kegan and Lisa Lahey, in their brilliant book *Immunity to Change* provide insight into this topic, showing how our "hidden commitments" (e.g., wanting to have control, put your stamp on things) build up our immunity to change.[36] This immunity extends to personal forms of change, including and especially our leader development and growth. Bottom line: it will be difficult, if not impossible, to gain these types of insights about yourself without doing some deep reflection made possible by authenticity and vulnerability.

Not only is reflection critical so you can slow down and study yourself, but projecting into the future is only possible with some vulnerability and thought. For example, I had a leader I was working with closely for several months. He was a great client because he was willing to put in the work to try out new things to help bring him into alignment with who he wanted to be. However, my job was to help him keep his eye on where he was going by getting him to reflect on the "begin with the end in mind" and "what does success look like" type reflection points.

The final piece to Shallow Frenzy that bears discussion is that people who fit this profile often are frustrated by the

---

[36] Kegan, Robert, & Lahey, Lisa. *Immunity to Change*. Harvard Business Review Press, 2009.

process of deep work and often the people who undertake it. My experience with developing leaders is that there is resistance to the process of change almost as much as the change itself. You can become frustrated, for example, if you are in an accountability relationship with someone who has been moving slower than you perceive they should be, or that you perceive you are. After all, you are wanting to try anything to get better, so you fear you will be slowed down by their process.

To help someone demonstrating Shallow Frenzy,

- Provide external checks and balances to keep them on track for genuine and sustained growth (i.e., ensure development fits what they need, while being sensitive to what they're interested in).

- Offer frequent, objective assessments and evaluations of their skills and growth needs.

- Ensure they are deliberate and intentional in their practice (i.e., emphasize quality, not just quantity, of knowledge, skills).

- Encourage ongoing reflection of acquired knowledge and skills by framing how learning fits with goals and interests.

- Build in measures of accountability with check-ins and reviews.

- Drive them back to the "why" of their learning and development.

- Provide a dose of reality about the challenges in consistent, sustainable behavior and leadership change.

- Be a role model of slow, intentional development through journaling and self-reflection.

Authentic Development: Willing to Act, True to Areas for Growth ("The Learner")

So far, you've read about the three profiles of leader development. These profiles depict tendencies and behaviors. They all have their downsides, as well as things outside and inside a leader's control that lead them to act out the tendencies you read about. At this point, I want to be clear that, yes, Authentic Development is the goal. At the same time, no one is perfect. While you read these profiles, **treat Authentic Development as aspirational and give yourself some grace as you read about it**. In the same way that I can watch great speakers like the late Steve Jobs or motivational speaker Simon Sinek and learn from them without being intimidated by them, my hope is the same for you. See this final profile and set of behaviors as your goal. Indeed, it might just be "what success looks like" for you.

People in the Authentic Development profile are true Learners. They are both highly open to and aware of their need for development and constant improvement *and* they are highly committed to acting on those authentic areas for development. Yes, it is a both/and proposition. They do the hard, sweaty work to practice vulnerability, authenticity, reflection, and projection, *and* they practice small, measure that progress, hold themselves accountable, and let others keep them accountable. They take feedback and truly consider it. They tell their emotion-oriented part of their brain that responds negatively to feedback to hush so they can process the feedback rationally. Even if they are suspicious of the accuracy of the feedback, they appreciate the person who delivered it, and they use feedback as an opportunity to connect with them to learn more and build the relationship.

Learners take tools like the Mental Replay reflection activity and use it consistently, sharing what they find with others. More than that, they bring others—whether they lead the team or not—into the journey and practice that form of "gamefilming" together. This form of social learning, which we'll discuss more in Chapter 12, builds relationships and strengthens the bond of teams around shared goals, wins, and challenges. Speaking of teams, Learners and those committed to Authentic Development take the time to go to the next level with their accountability by developing other people. They know that when they get better, they have the opportunity to help others do the same. Indeed, a rising tide lifts all boats.

If you are in the profile of Authentic Development, you work to get your hands on lots of development research and tools *and* you use that info to reflect on your current work environment, feedback you've given, and who you want to be. You consider everything in light of your I Am and I Will statements (Chapter 9). What fits? What doesn't fit but nevertheless, challenges you to think differently and bigger about yourself and your leadership? In other words, you're intentional about measuring your progress periodically and sharing it with others.

Beyond these specific practices, a work in progress is your identity—it's who you are. I had a mentor early on in my career who used to say, "everything is just grist for the mill." I've always loved that saying as a metaphor because if you work in a leadership role or even if you're not quite there, but you work around people, you have virtually unlimited opportunities to work on yourself. You *learn* to see everything as useful experiences, material, and knowledge for growth. As you go about your leadership and influencing others, you are intentional about mining for data (Chapter 6) to use for your growth and others' benefit.

On a broader, leadership lifespan level, you see past experiences, including and especially the negative ones, in a positive light. After all, they teach you a lot about how to get better. You've developed a positive and productive relationship with your emotions. You might have felt embarrassed or frustrated by how you acted in the past, but you've learned to use those emotions to get better, and help you make that feeling–thinking–doing connection.

Recently I was talking to a student about an advising issue. The student was having the hardest time understanding something that I thought was basic. At one point, I got frustrated with him and said, "I've given you all the information, but I can't understand this for you." It was one of those things where what I said was technically true and valid. But *how* I said it was a problem. As I "reviewed the tape" on that occurrence, I just really didn't like how I showed up to that student. See, I can communicate that message and achieve my goal of helping the students think for themselves without coming across as a jerk. For the most part, I'm a nice guy. In fact, sometimes my niceness gets in the way of my ability to get firm when I need to. The issue for me is balance. I struggle to balance toughness and tact. As a result, I can go from nice to jerk in about five seconds, either verbally or nonverbally, and most of the time both. Unfortunately, or fortunately, I have a lot of those negative experiences to pull from, reflect on, and learn from. If treated right and processed productively, they just give me more ways to get better. Again, my feelings help me think, my thoughts help me in my actions. The beauty in this perspective is also that you learn to learn from even the positive experiences. You don't become complacent. Instead, you take note of the good and the positive "triggers" to help you know what to keep doing.

To help someone demonstrating Authentic Development,

- Encourage and support their ongoing development efforts, avoiding the tendency to let their needs go unmet as you help others.

- Partner them with others who need help with either openness or action, while being careful not to burn them out.

- Provide flexible development opportunities.

- Offer the opportunity to teach, coach, and train others in the organization on sustained, authentic development.

- Equip them with tools and resources necessary to continue to sharpen their skills and broaden their opportunities.

- Seek their advice on best practices for learning and development.

Model of Authentic Leader Development

Willful Stubbornness	**Authentic Development**	
Oblivious Apathy	**Shallow Frenzy**	

HIGH ↑

Openness to Development

LOW ↓

LOW ← *Action* Oriented → HIGH

Personalize It

Part I: Identify

Take the blank 2x2 model below and fill it in based on behaviors you have witnessed either in yourself or others in your development journey. Review the examples offered in the chapter to get you started.

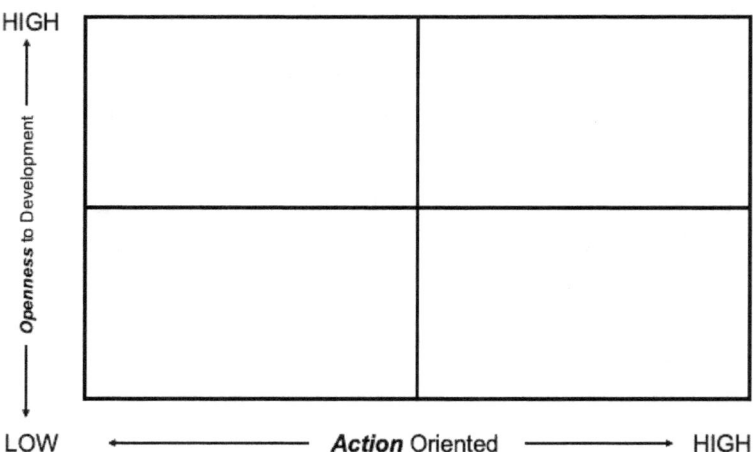

Part II: Support

How can you support someone you know who may fit into one of the profiles below in order to help them move toward more sustained, authentic development? How would you advise them to change their approach so they can be more effective?

Oblivious Apathy

Willful Stubbornness

Shallow Frenzy

SECTION V

Sustaining Growth for a Lifetime

I'll go out on a limb here and guess that if you're putting in the work to grow and develop, you'd like to be able to sustain those gains. Right? After all, no one likes to lose a bunch of weight, only to see it come right back. The same goes for your gains as a leader. The tricky part about leadership growth and development is that there are so many dynamic factors that make it hard to sustain. Remember, a core premise of this book is authenticity—seeing yourself as a work in progress. In this final section, the last two chapters lay out some ideas for how to maximize learning outside of and between formal training/coaching experiences and how to make developing others part of your development plan. Let's finish strong, shall we?

12

Maximize Life Outside the 10%

A common challenge that all leader developers face, whether we're talking about coaching or training, is how to drive and ensure ongoing development outside the formal development setting. For example, if you're in a one-hour coaching session with me, we can cover a lot of ground in that time frame, but the magic happens outside of that setting—where you really need the skills you're developing. If you're trying to be more assertive, we can practice and role play, but the payoff comes when you practice being more assertive with Jay, your direct report whom you need to challenge to do better quality work. Similarly, if I'm your facilitator for your company's five-month, 10-session leadership academy, what really matters is what you do with the content between sessions. This is the age-old challenge of transferring your learning back to where it counts.

Neuroscience research shows clearly that one of the key elements in effective learning and development is spacing,[37] that is, taking time between learning events/sessions to practice, try stuff out. However, a vastly underutilized tool I urge you to add to your tool kit is some form of reflection and follow-up between sessions about that practice. To reiterate, in my experience, people don't do this nearly enough. I get it. If you're a leader in a multi-session leadership academy, that is enough of a time commitment by itself. Chances are you might have some homework between sessions, so if you add it up, it's a heavy weight to add to your already full schedule. I hear you but I implore you to not miss this important step.

I've briefly alluded to the 70-20-10 model of training and learning in previous chapters, but in case you're not familiar with it, here's a primer so you can see the power in the work between sessions. Here's what it shows us about how leaders learn:

- 10% comes from formal coursework and training.

- 20% comes from developmental relationships.

- 70% comes from challenging experiences and assignments (i.e., on-the-job work).

If these numbers are correct, and my experience and years of research shows they are, then **your formal training and coaching sessions will play a significantly small role in your development**. The power of between-session work is it brings the 20% and 70% together by harnessing collaboration and on-the-job learning. That is, when you make a

---

[37] France, Nicholas. *Variability and Spaced Learning Key to Enhanced Memory.* Neuroscience News, 2024.

commitment to do something with what you learned in a session and you share that with someone who then keeps you accountable and shares their experiences, you're simply much more likely to put it into practice where it counts: on the job. **Between-session work creates a virtuous circle of learning—reflecting—sharing—practicing**.

The simplest way to add between-session work to your routine is a journaling practice. In Chapter 10, we saw how to drive self-accountability via journaling, but I want to add a wrinkle here. I encourage journaling and utilizing a discussion board or listserv with others, notably with others in the academy or with your coach. There are several ways to use the board effectively. We'll explore two ways to do it, with some examples. The examples here are long but hopefully they provide you with concrete ways to put them into practice.

Let's take a common example where you have a training session and have two or three weeks between sessions. First, at the end of a training session you can make a commitment to emphasize certain skills or mindsets in the coming weeks. In this example, with the help of your trainer/facilitator, you are deciding what you want to focus on. Say the broad topic of the session was "conscious communication." The emphasis here is on being more mindful of the mindsets, values, and tendencies of those you're communicating with, and your own as well. With that knowledge, your goal is to better adapt your style of communication with those you lead. You can make a commitment to be more present, and better hone your listening skills so you can tune in to more accurately understand your people. Active listening was a topic you discussed in the workshop, so you decide that that will be your focal point for the next two weeks. You decide to post at least two examples each week of where you've practiced some of the techniques you learned in the session. The goal then is to have others in your cohort share their examples and experiences so the rich discussions that (hopefully) happened in the training session continue in the discussion board. Here's what an entry might look like:

Jeremy's Post:

- Personal insights working through conscious communications.

- My communication skills are situation specific:

  - I am often told that I am a great communicator, but the reality is this is only when I am in a favorable mode/situation. For example:

    - I present well in individual and group settings—most of this is the ability to synthesize difficult concepts and discuss in understandable ways. I dialogue well and connect well in one-on-one situations.

- The alternative is I have communication shortfalls when not in a favorable mode:

  - One of my communication problems is turning on my presence/conscious communication (e.g., if I don't feel the topic is directly relevant to my work).

  - When someone interrupts me, I have a hard time switching modes/tasks.

  - When in a larger group setting, I struggle to turn active listening on.

The above post is a lengthier example of how to journal in between sessions in order to state your commitments and progress. Also, it's not the length of your posts that matter. What matters is that you are sharing something. Working through different examples as in the above post will only add to your learning by giving you more to emphasize throughout the weeks between sessions. But this is about your intentionality, which I defined earlier as "setting your mind to something." **Intentionality is about consciously bringing your awareness to something or back to something**. The between-session posts help you bring your awareness back to what you're trying to improve on, when your awareness is most likely on the work you're paid to do, understandably so. For the record, a post like the one above can also be an example of something you could write in your personal development journal if you're learning by yourself, so the same exercise works even if you're not going through a learning journey with a cohort.

Here's an example of a shorter but still impactful post, along with a response from another leader, Dan, in your training cohort:

Jeremy's Post:

Some present goals for Jeremy:

- A list of communication and mindfulness reminders to use along with journaling.

- A list of situations that regularly occur and how I should reset and handle them (one team member tends to barge in, another always just waits at my door, etc.).

- More practice on resetting: stop-breathe-regroup.

Dan's Post:

> Jeremy, thank you for mentioning the "resetting" practice. I had a conversation with my 8-year-old the other day where I had to use this. The conversation wasn't going well but I did the reset, and it really did help. I didn't think I would use this stuff at home, but it totally worked!

In the above, short examples, you have Jeremy specifically identifying things he wants to work on and Dan following up with how he has used the practices as well. **Specificity followed by encouragement is a potent two-step method for development.**

A second method you can utilize is to have your trainer or coach drive your points of emphasis in between sessions. For example, let's say you recently learned about different mindsets and worldviews, all which impact how we act and interact with others. Our mindsets connect to our values, beliefs, priorities, and much more. If this was your emphasis, a discussion post from your trainer could read something like this:

Trainer/Coach Post:

- Choose one experience to participate in that simulates traveling and immersing yourself into the mindset you are least comfortable with. Spend time with the people there, be a learner, actively listen for meaning, and participate in customs that stretch your boundaries—when in Rome!

For example:

• Attend a church service of a different denomination you're used to. If you're Baptist, attend a Pentecostal service or vice-versa. If you're Church of Christ, attend a service at an African Methodist Episcopal (AME) church.

• Try a boxing or mixed-martial arts class or attend a similar event.

One or more of those should push your buttons! Please let me know your gameplan should you choose to accept this mission. I'm happy to help you pick your poison :)

Two positive outcomes could follow this, and ideally both will. First, your fellow trainees comment on any similar experiences they've had that you're committing to. Second, and perhaps most importantly, following your experience you committed to, you come back to the discussion board and share what happened, or you share the next time you're together with your peers. Discussion boards capitalize on two important ingredients in sustained development: spacing and collaboration. You have time between sessions to practice, then by sharing, you collaborate with others to hold you accountable.

In summary, I encourage you to utilize discussion boards in between your training or coaching sessions. It works whether you or your peers drive your points of emphasis, or your trainer/coach drives them. The posts don't have to be long; they just need to happen. I'll close this chapter with a few guidelines and suggestions for making the most out of discussion boards.

Be Specific

Avoid writing things such as "be more conscious with my communication." Although being more conscious is a good thing, it's vague and largely unhelpful in terms of you making changes. Ask yourself what conscious communication would look like for you. Do you need to turn off your notifications on your phone and watch? Do you need to turn your phone face down when someone walks in? (For the record, the answer to both preceding questions is yes!) Do you need to work on asking better questions to help with active listening? **Specific actions are concrete; concrete actions can be put into practice.**

Make a Commitment

The magic in the above example post of attending a religious service or event is that there's a commitment. It's an activity with a fixed outcome—you will know something happened. Likewise, make a commitment to yourself and your peers in the discussion board. It might not be a specific event like the ones referenced above, but you can commit to holding a one-on-one with a direct report you've been avoiding that difficult conversation with. As you can probably see, being specific and making a commitment are connected, perhaps even co-requisites. In other words, it's hard to commit to something vague, and vice-versa. **Specificity is the ground in which commitments can grow and thrive.**

Collaborate

Finally, make sure others are with you on the journey. Commit to each other that you're going to respond to one another's posts, share wins and challenges, and nudge your peers to be their best. If you're utilizing a discussion board or something like it in a one-on-one discussion coaching partnership, establish expectations with your coach early on about how often you will post and his/her role in responding to your posts. Collaboration in a discussion board is about holding each other accountable and supporting one another. Collaboration and accountability go together just like specificity and commitment. **Collaboration breeds accountability; accountability enriches collaboration**.

I know work between sessions sounds daunting. The training/coaching time commitment itself is already significant. But I can't encourage or challenge you enough to add this to your practice. I promise, if you give it time and follow the guidelines above, it will pay off. Remember, by working on things in between session, you're making the most out of the 90% of life and work where real learning takes place.

Another method of between-session follow-up is conversations with your leader. Hopefully, if you're engaged in a learning journey of some sort, be it a leadership academy, a series of "elective" courses at your company, or a coaching partnership, you have some sort of follow-up and follow through with your boss. This follow-up can be formal or informal, but like discussion boards, it just needs to happen. Some of the biggest questions I get about this are: How often should we meet? What do we talk about? What questions can/should I ask? Where do we meet?

Many of the details are best worked out between you and your leader, but my best advice is to find a place, time, and routine that works for you where two key ingredients can thrive: vulnerability and honesty.

Here's a quick personal story to illustrate. I love having conversations with my kids in the car. Most of the time, they're in the backseat, so we don't have direct eye contact. If the topic calls for it, I'll have my oldest ride up front with me so we can be closer. Even still, I'm looking forward (mostly!) and she's sometimes looking at me, sometimes looking forward. Recently I needed to have a conversation with her on a topic related to school safety. I was going to take her to voice lessons so I asked her to sit up front with me so we could talk. She probably sensed it was somewhat serious based on my tone, but still, there's just something freeing, unassuming, and real about it being in the car. Yes, there are absolutely times when my wife and I will sit down with our girls at home, eye-to-eye with zero distractions. We do it often when the topic warrants it. Having the safety conversation in the car allowed me to walk that delicate line between being honest and real without scaring her unnecessarily. I want her to know about it without being so petrified she can't think. Do any parents out there know what I mean?

I work closely with a leader who has a lot of "windshield time" because he drives a lot for work. He often has conversations with his boss there. It's convenient for his schedule, and they've developed a rapport that is crucial for growth and development. For you, it might be at the local coffee shop, the company lunchroom, the tavern down the road, or a weekly Teams or Zoom call.

Here's my point. **Have follow-up conversations with your leader when, where, and how you can.** One caveat: like my example with my kids, there might be times when a more intentional and serious setting is called for. The medium and where a conversation happens often communicates a message by itself.[38] If a serious issue or challenge comes up in a training or coaching session that you need to address with

---

[38] For more on this idea, see Media Richness Theory.

your leader, a formal sit-down might be warranted. Or, if you are a leader whose employee is attending a training or getting coaching, an issue might be brought to your attention that needs to be corrected. My advice here is to feel it out and apply situation-specific strategies to know when and where to have the conversation.

Personalize It

Map out what the 70-20-10 method might look like for you.

- 10%: What are the formal trainings and resources you can use to help you develop your skills and reach your goals?

- 20%: Who are the relationships you can leverage to help you develop your skills and reach your goals?

- 70%: Identify examples of how you can leverage on-the-job training to help you develop your skills and reach your goals.

How will you track and measure your progress as you are practicing on the job?

Where and how can you utilize between-session journaling and follow-up to help you develop your skills and reach your goals?

Bonus: Start an online thread with an accountability partner you're completing training with. Reflect on your takeaways and insights below:

13

D.I.Y. & Grow Others

My wife and I love doing projects around the house. We are D.I.Y.-ers.[39] We've owned four houses together and we've always done lots of projects. We bought our first house together, after about 15 months of marriage, in a hip and up-and-coming area of Milwaukee called Wauwatosa. We bought it back in 2011 when it was clearly a buyer's market. The home had been renovated and flipped but there were many things we wanted to do to put our touches on it. Our first project we did together was to finish the basement. It was a big undertaking and since it was our first, we learned a lot together. Well, to be fair, I learned a lot. See, my wife Brooke is an incredible D.I.Y.-er. She can build and do just about anything. Plumbing, electrical, woodworking—you name it, she can do it. Remember back in Chapter 8 I talked

---

[39]   To those unfamiliar, D.I.Y. means Do It Yourself.

about my father-in-law? Now you know where she gets it! She's creative and has the chops to see her vision to fruition. Me? Well, I'm just the labor on all our projects. If she needs a nail cut with a pair of pliers, I'm the guy. Cutting things out with a reciprocating saw? Put me in. Lifting heavy boards? Yep. Beyond that, I have a hard time seeing her vision of what we're building until it's just about done, and I'm hardly exaggerating on that. Throughout the years, we've taken on big projects such as finishing a basement, knocking out a wall to expand a master bathroom, turning a room into a classroom for homeschool, building a playhouse from scratch for our girls, and building a duck enclosure for our ducks. We've also done small(ish) projects including tiling, installing backsplashes, building built-in cabinets, and crafting a table for our deck.

The above examples help draw out two important lessons for your personal and leader development. First, **sometimes your work on yourself will be a small project. Other times call for what feels like a total overhaul**. Second, like my wife and I, there are probably people in your life who you can help grow and who can help you grow. This final chapter explores both of these to give you even more ways to take what you've learned in this book, compound the effects, and make growth sustain for the long haul.

"Never stop improving." For years, this was the slogan used by the home improvement giant, Lowe's. I find this to be a helpful mantra for us as leaders to live by as well. After all, throughout this book I've defined authenticity as *seeing yourself as a work in progress*. Like a home, where you're often improving, building, and fixing stuff, if you're honest, there's always something you can be doing with your leadership and you generally. Even if you get to the point where you've "mastered" or "finished" work on one area, situations change, and people change. You get promoted and asked to take on more. You're a good speaker, but this next audience you're speaking to intimidates you more than usual. Or, more broadly, your industry is probably changing. **As your scope of control grows and business changes, it will necessitate constant improvement.**

With that in mind, think about what a "small" renovation project might look like for you. What's the personal and leader development equivalent to a backsplash or building a table? Side note: I'm sensitive to the fact that, if you're not big on D.I.Y. projects, installing a backsplash or building a table might not seem small at all! It's all relative.

But sticking with the size and scale metaphor here, a small personal project might be working on blocking distractions so you can focus more. A few years back, I coached an executive at a nonprofit who was working on this very thing. Blocking out distractions was a small part of a larger project of time and task management and being more available to her team. She just couldn't get out of scramble mode so she could really scale up her efforts to execute more effectively. To be clear, I'm not saying blocking things out is easy, but it's relatively small in the sense that it's concrete. Reducing the number of push notifications you receive on your phone is a simple, albeit not easy, concrete action.

Do some reflecting with me here. What are other, "small" projects for you? Do any of these below ring true? As you review the examples below, make your own quick list of small projects using the Personalize It prompts at the end of the chapter.

- Setting short 1-1 meetings with your team.

- Asking more powerful questions in meetings.

- Improving your eye contact in presentations.

- Becoming a better storyteller in presentations.

- Communicating with empathy and concern.

- Practicing active listening.

- Practicing "counterfactual" thinking in decision making.

- Holding a coaching conversation with a team member.

- Conducting a Mental Replay to better understand your reactions and emotions.

- Learning how to give behavior-based feedback.

It bears repeating here that some of you might review this list and think many of these seem like big undertakings. Indeed, at first, they might very well be, depending on you and your personality. For instance, I worked with an executive one time for whom "communicating with empathy and concern" was a massive challenge because, admittedly, she's "not a very empathetic person." My point for you though is that **by "small" I mean that what you are trying to work on has concrete, actionable steps attached to it.** For instance, I worked with her on planning 1-2 simple questions she can ask of her team members that communicate care and concern such as, *"what have you tried so far and how can I support you in that?"*

Another way to understand a "small" project is by how quickly you might expect to practice and see results (i.e., quick wins). Leading through simple questions such as the ones above is highly actionable right away, and she could see results from that quickly. When Brooke and I do a backsplash project, it's rewarding because we can usually start and finish it in a weekend. Saturday morning the wet saw gets fired up and by Monday I'm sipping my coffee, admiring our work. So too with some of these "small" leadership projects. "Nothing motivates like progress," the saying goes. The beauty of these small leadership D.I.Y. projects is that they offer a sense of progress.

At the same time, **as you learn to be vulnerable and reflect more, other things you need to work on are going to be bigger**. Whereas the small projects are typically action-oriented, concrete, and behavior based, many of the big projects are identity-based. They just see the light of day in the form of certain behaviors.

At the very least, our struggles with them have identity shifts that need to happen so we can improve. For example, I worked with an executive closely for many months on his delegation or lack thereof. Over the course of a few coaching sessions, we worked on techniques to help him hand things off more. About one-third of the way through our partnership, he admitted something to me. When he said it, I don't think he realized what an ah-ha moment it was. To paraphrase, he told me that in a previous role as C.E.O. he had "been burned" when he gave some things up and thus lost trust in people. Consequently, he has been protective over his role and responsibilities ever since. This led him to be protective down to the smallest detail of not wanting people to have login information, as just one example. From that point on, we redirected our efforts—his efforts—toward him noticing and "data mining" (see Chapter 6) for when he feels that protective instinct creeping in, thereby getting in the way of his need to delegate. We developed a simple tool kit of self-reflection questions he asked at key points to help overcome this challenge. For this executive, he had some deep identity work that needed to happen before he had a shot at changing his behavior.

Importantly, note that had he not reflected and opened up about being burned in a previous role, we wouldn't have been able to know, let alone get to the root of his troubles in the first place. This demonstrates the power of reflection and having someone you can talk to and keep you accountable (e.g., a coach, close colleague, or friend).

Just as we did with the smaller projects, do some reflecting. What are the big projects you might want to work on? Do any of the following ring true?

- Getting better audience engagement in presentations.

- Learning to delegate more effectively.

- Empowering your team.

- Developing a growth mindset.

- Becoming a more intentional networker.

- Learning the business more thoroughly.

- Boosting the morale of your team.

- Building trust with your team.

- Learning to take better ownership over parts of the business you might not be interested in.

- Learning to keep your commitments.

- Building your brand as a leader.

- Learning to practice emotional intelligence.

As you can probably imagine based on many of my recommendations up to this point, I don't advise trying to take on too many of these big projects at once. I see these big projects as "seasonal" projects. Just like my wife and I might do one big project at the start of spring and one in fall, just one of these big identity-based projects might be something you commit to for a whole season, maybe a whole year. Yes, you will look for wins and other markers of success to help you measure your progress monthly or maybe quarterly; but your time horizon is much longer on these. Not sure where to start? Refer back to your Mental Replay, Gap Analysis, and I Am statements, just to name a few. (As a reminder, you can find a complete list of tools and frameworks covered throughout the book in the appendix at the end.)

Some of our big development projects must be reflected on in and of themselves before we can attempt behavior change, as illustrated by the earlier example about delegation. My client had to recognize and get to the root of his struggles to delegate. That said, my recommendation when you review the big projects is, once you feel like you get to the root of the challenge the big project presents, is to ask yourself one simple question: *What are the small projects I can start with so I can start to tackle the big ones?*

To use another example, let's say you're wanting to learn to practice emotional intelligence (EI). Considering there are five components to EI (self-awareness, self-regulation, empathy, motivation, social skills), it's safe to say that that would be a big project. Any one of the components of EI is a project all by itself. My advice if I were coaching you would be for you to start small and learn to practice self-awareness. For example, you could begin conducting a Mental Replay after each of your 1-1 meetings with direct reports for the next four weeks. So, again, it's a big project but with small projects that you can start with to help you tackle it.

Try the following simple exercise to help you get there:

My big project for January–July this year is

_____

My small project I will commit to first is

_____

Do it *Yourself?*

In many ways, the metaphor of D.I.Y. is a misnomer. If you've been reading closely, you know I don't recommend making leader development a solo enterprise. In reality then, you're not really doing it all yourself. The point to emphasize though is, **much of the sweaty, hard work of personal development must be done by you, behind the scenes.** Analogous to hiring a personal trainer to help you work out, she is going to depend on you to do the work outside of the training sessions and not ruin your progress by decisions you make at the dinner table.

As you progress in your leader development, I hope you'll be intentional about bringing others into your journey (see Chapter 10 on how to practice "other" accountability) so you can grow more effectively. Leadership happens in the context of other people, so it makes sense that leadership development should as well. The additional benefit of bringing others into your journey is that you get the opportunity to help them grow. See, when my wife and I do projects, she is almost always the project lead. For the sake of aesthetics and structural integrity, trust me, you want her as the project lead.

But the beauty of us working together is two-fold. First, I grow in the process as I build and sharpen my skill set. Second, and I argue more importantly, we grow closer together. I'm a believer that all couples should take on D.I.Y. projects of some sort, or some big project together early on in their marriage. Nothing bonds people, from couples to coworkers to teams, like solving a problem or overcoming a challenge together, thereby capitalizing on the power of the shared struggle.[40] Likewise, all leaders and their direct reports should see that relationship as one of mutual growth. I don't mean the boss tells the direct report what to do and what to work on. I mean that leaders and direct reports work on things *together* through vulnerability, authenticity, reflection, practice, measurement, and accountability.

Leader, one of your greatest responsibilities—and I believe joys—will come when you help others grow and develop. But you might be wondering, how can I do that? In the last part of this final chapter, I offer you two perspectives to guide you in growing others.

Your first practice, and this will sound simple, is through modeling. You are going to talk about your areas for development (i.e., weaknesses) as well as what you're doing to get better, what you continue to struggle with, and so on. You are going to model vulnerability and authenticity, and you can do so without compromising your credibility. If your people see you as a leader who knows her stuff (i.e., your business acumen is sharp), then you will only enhance your credibility by being real. If you happened to skip ahead or just need a refresher, refer to Chapters 4 and 5 on vulnerability and authenticity, respectively, for more on that.

---

[40] Heath, Chip, & Heath, Dan. *The Power of Moments: Why Certain Experiences have Extraordinary Impact.* Simon & Schuster, 2017.

Modeling has numerous other benefits as well, including, but not limited to, helping your people manage their work and workload.[41] For example, if you have a direct report who is wanting to gain a better sense of "balance" in his work and life, as difficult or sometimes impossible as that is, he will benefit most from seeing how you do that. If he sees you checking and responding to email at all hours, let alone if he thinks you expect that of him, that will work against his goals of gaining better balance. Instead, communicate to him and your whole team that you expect them to be fully present with their families at home, just like you need him to be present when focusing on an important task at work. Talk about how although you need him to be fully present at work, you know he has a family at home, so when things come up at home, you expect him to just be honest with you and proactive about communicating his needs. Act out the behaviors and talk about it honestly. It's a both/and proposition. As these conversations unfold, you might find it helpful to help him reframe what he's trying to accomplish as "work-life integration." You show him and talk about how by focusing and giving his attention to his work at work, he can then be more fully present at home. The reverse is true. For more formal methods, you can advocate for policies that ensure your team feels safe to be "off the clock."

The second method for helping grow others, and this is a close cousin to the first, is to facilitate social learning. As much as people might want to appear independent and not moved by what other people do (i.e., "going along with the crowd"), social norms are an extremely potent factor

---

[41]　"Who Is Responsible for Protecting Work-Life Balance? It Depends Who You Ask." Fast Company, 2022.

in behavior change and growth.[42] Put simply, when people look around and see other people learning, growing, changing, struggling but winning, and so on, they will be more likely to follow suit. A macro-level version of this is what the Neuroleadership Institute refers to as "everyone-to-everyone learning" wherein entire teams, units, or organizations go through the same learning experiences together.[43] Thanks to emerging neuroscience research, **we know that our brains are most impacted (i.e., we're learning) when learning happens in a social context**. Interpersonal connections are activated, accountability is more likely, and people form bonds with each other that will ultimately make growth and real, sustained change more likely.

The take-home point? You're the leader, so lead the way. You might not be in a position, due to size, scale, or your budget, to have your whole team take part in a big training initiative. But that's not the point. You can make a difference right where you are with little to no budget at all just by showing what you're working on and facilitating learning and growth groups. Sit down with all members of your team and talk through what they are working to develop. Take tools from this book (e.g., Mental Replay; Chapter 6) and work through them together. Have everyone on or in your team form their leadership "I Am" statements (Chapter 9), share them, and then facilitate accountability conversations moving forward to ensure people are true to who they said they are. If you are not in a formal leadership position at all, you

---

[42] "The Most Surprising Reason People Change." Neuroleadership Institute, 2022.

[43] "It's Time for a New Approach to Change: Everyone-to-Everyone Learning." Neuroleadership Institute, 2024.

can take the lead in starting these efforts. Form a resource group dedicated to personal growth in development.

Whether you are leading this as the leader of the team or as a team member, you will serve yourself and the team well because the outcomes are more sustained development, as well as a boost in morale and belongingness. Just like my wife and I grow closer by struggling through projects, we get closer as we get to see and enjoy the fruits of our labor. I don't want to do D.I.Y. projects truly alone—no matter how small or large. And the truth is, *everyone* is better off if I don't.

Personalize It

What are your "small projects" you need to work on/build?

What are your "big projects" you need to work on/build?

My big project for January–July (or similar timeframe) this year is

My small project I will commit to first is

I can help grow others by better modeling _____
for my people.

This will help them in their own development because

If you are a leadership development practitioner in charge of designing training programs in your organization, what are ways you can use the concepts in this chapter to innovate and effectively develop people (e.g., modeling, social learning, everyone-to-everyone learning).

Conclusion

"The most meaningful growth is not building
our careers–it's building our character."
–Adam Grant, *Hidden Potential*

I write this final chapter at the end of another fall semester of getting to teach, advise, and develop students and leaders. I've been teaching in higher education since 2006 and honestly it still excites me like it did back when I started, as a graduate teaching assistant.

Heading into this Winter break though, something is different. I just recently accepted a new role at Belmont University, overseeing leadership development across campus. Specifically, I'll be the Director of Character-Centered Leadership Development. As I've written throughout this book, leadership is about learning and growth—we learn and grow as our leadership scope and challenges grow. I'll be moving out of teaching full-time in the classroom and into an administrative leadership position.

Dear reader, honestly, I'm experiencing the full range of emotions as I make this move. I'm excited, a little nervous, eager to get started. Mostly though, I'm just excited. As I wrote in the introduction, there's a leader in all of us who we've never met. I'm about to step into a new season of discovering who that leader is. And a year from now, there will be a new leader I'll need to welcome and get to know. Someone reading this right now is in that exact season of change and new leadership roles. We're in this together. I'm a work in progress.

In my experience getting to develop thousands of leaders in my career, I've found that the primary emphasis is, indeed, as Adam Grant's quote alludes to, often on career development or career progression. Or it's on leadership effectiveness and execution, and the skills needed for both. Those are fine and good things. But they are only as good as the self-leadership that accompanies it. And that's where character comes in. The character development that's absolutely essential for self-leadership are things like honesty, humility, resiliency, and accountability.

At the outset I laid out four goals I had for you in writing this book: to know yourself better, adopt a work-in-progress mindset, emphasize self-leadership as much as anything else you're responsible for, and teach what you know to others. As you reflect on those four goals, and considering everything you read and learned in this book, I hope you see that character development is a critical part.

As you learn, grow, try new techniques and tools, win, and fail, you'll need to continue to be honest with yourself about what's working and what's not working. Just keep reflecting, just keep trying, just keep getting better. Your people will admire you for it and will model it for themselves. They'll execute more effectively and lead others better.

My final invitation is to share your stories with me. I've shared some examples of leaders I've been blessed to work with in the past, and I pray I get to hear your wins and even setbacks too. Getting to partner with leaders is a great joy, and I can't imagine doing anything else. Your stories inspire me–the good, bad, tough, and beautiful. Let's keep working at it together and seeing ourselves as a work in progress. In the end, that's how we discover the authentic leader we never knew.

Acknowledgments

This book is a culmination and indeed a celebration of many years of thinking, reflecting, practicing, and some writing. It's ultimately a testament to God's goodness, provision, and faithfulness in my life. To God be the glory. I get to do what I do because of the gifts He's given me. Ephesians 2:10 says that we are Christ's workmanship, His handiwork. He indeed crafted me, so I pray I make the most of every opportunity to show His glory in my work. As I stated at the beginning, I believe He created all of us to serve others, and for many of us, we're blessed that that takes the form of leadership in some capacity, perhaps formally. And I've been blessed, as are all leaders, to have an incredible cast of people around me to share it.

Brooke, you are a daily reminder of God's goodness, patience, and character in my life. My ideas and aspirations are sometimes as wild as my voice is loud, and you stick with me, stick by me every step of the way. You question when it's the right time to do so before I go off the rails but do so with a conversational intelligence that is truly a gift. You are an encourager. There is no one who listens better than you. Period! You speak and write well; you teach our kids;

you pray with random people at Walmart; you do plumbing, electrical and anything else a D.I.Y-er could dream of. You are truly the Last of the Mohicans. Most impressively, you love God and your family with a tenacity that is unmatched. You are a fierce woman of God, and I am so blessed to do life with you. You are my partner in crime (P.I.C.)[44] and shotgun rider!

Emma and Lennon, you fill our house with so much fun, joy, and silliness. I pray that you read this and look back on it and are proud of your dad. Mostly, I pray that you can confidently say that I lived up to who I said I want to be—present at all times with the ones God has blessed under my care. You inspire me to be the best version of the leader God created me to be and model godly leadership at home. Keep dreaming big, girls. You will have no bigger cheerleaders than your mom and me. I'll love you as long as Jesus does—forever! And remember, you too are a work in progress, always!

Mom and Dad, you taught me to love God, be kind to others, and work hard. Mom, I remember you waking me up for school by spraying water in my face when I was impossible to rouse. I hated it at the time, but you were teaching me the importance of getting up and showing up. You bring a zest, passion, and care to everything you do, and I thank you for modeling that for me. Dad, you modeled how to work hard to provide for your family *and* be fully there, never missing big (and small) moments. Doing both is the hard part, but you did it so well. I thank you for modeling what presence looks like. Later in life, you've become an awesome sounding board for so many crazy things I've wanted to do. I thank you for your patient listening and invaluable questions-over-advice approach to things.

---

44   For the record, we've committed no actual crimes ☺

Kevin and Beth, even though you're technically my "in-laws," you're truly family, and I can't imagine my life without you. Your ongoing support, guidance, and prayers over me and my work is absolutely priceless. Kevin, you're always there to provide a much-needed dose of calm and perspective to help me think through things. Beth, you're a powerhouse mom and nurse, and someone who shows Jesus to the world in everything you do. I love you both so much!

I'm thankful for my students, whom I've had the pleasure of serving in higher education since 2006. You inspire me to be and do more. Many of our classroom experiences have been the ground in which the ideas in this book have been tested.

Speaking of students, to Haley Charlton and Bailey Johnson, thank you for your great work interviewing the leaders featured in the "Leader Lessons" section. To Pearson Ezell and Morgan Bagus, you kept me focused and on track with all your excellent insights and encouragement. The world is in good hands with you future leaders at the helm!

To the authentic leaders I've been so blessed to train, speak to, and coach, you are a gift. I am inspired by your grit and determination to not only execute and be excellent at what you do, but also to work on yourself. Every tool, technique, and approach in this book has been tested, refined, and reworked in my 13+ years getting to work with leaders.

Mentioning specific people in a section like this is tricky business because I'm sure I'll forget someone, but here goes. To my colleagues at Marquette University and Belmont University, thank you for your support and for cheering me on while I worked to balance teaching and my training business. When I was a newly minted professor out of grad school at Purdue, Sarah Feldner, Scott D'Urso, and Erik Ugland in particular took me under their wing and had so many conversations that helped me get off on solid footing in my new role. Former Dean Lori Bergen helped me get adjusted to university life and supported so much of my travel and other ideas and projects I had going on. Most recently, thank you to my long-time chair at Belmont, Mary Vaughn for your support and guidance, and for being mindful of my work/life integration, including my long commute! Other people at Belmont supported my crazy ideas when I launched Two Heads Hot Sauce during that weird pandemic semester of fall 2020. Nathan Webb, you've been a constant colleague and friend, always there with an open ear for advice about anything. I'm excited for this next chapter!

Outside of Belmont, I have countless people to thank, but I'll name a few here. To Rand Stagen, thank you for letting me spend a summer with you and your incredible team of facilitators and coaches. I wrote about this in the introduction, but that experience was absolutely, 100% transformational for me. So much of what was written in this book directly or indirectly has roots there.

I have so many others that have, formally or informally formed my advisory board (see Adam Grant's *Think Again*). Craig Mueller, every time we talk, I get smarter and sharper. I love your perspective and commitment to leadership development that works. Matthew Millstein, you were there when I first started brainstorming for this book and for many of the innovative changes I made to my training business back in 2020. You are wise, way beyond your years. Adrian Davis, you are a boss of bosses. I love your heart for people and how you serve others.

To you, reader, thank you for investing your time and attention in this book. I pray it inspires, helps, and guides you into discovering the authentic leader God created you to be.

APPENDICES

APPENDIX A

Techniques & Tools: Further Readings & References List

I love tools, practices, and techniques, and trying out new things (in the context of authentic development, of course!). Below are the various approaches, tools, and techniques covered in the book. Others are based on things I've heard or read that have nothing to do with leader development, but I thought to myself "that would make a great practice for leaders." In these cases, I've had clients try them out, then I've refined them through trial and error and feedback.

Other tools and approaches are based on industry best practices and frameworks and solid evidence. In case you'd like to check out the science behind them or just learn more, here are some additional resources and readings for the things I have specific references to point you to.

Chapter 3: Who Before Do: Three Levels of Leadership

Three levels of leadership: Leading Self, Leading Others, Leading Initiatives (3 circle model)
Groeschel, Graig. "Leading Yourself."

Chapter 4: Be Vulnerable

Feeling → Thinking → Doing
Pink, Daniel. *The Power of Regret*. Riverhead Books, 2022.

Chapter 5: Be Authentic

Small and Large Questions
James, Hollis. *What Matters Most*. Gotham Books, 2009.

Triggers/Lifespan Approach
Avolio, Bruce. & Gardner, William. *Authentic Leadership Development: Getting To The Root Of Positive Forms of Leadership*. The Leadership Quarterly, 2005.
Hanks, Sarah. et al. *A Model of Leader Development Across the Lifespan*. Virginia Cooperative Extension, 2021.

Chapter 6: Reflect

Data Mining
Original practice, adapted from sermon by Pastor Brandon Petty, Generation Church.

Mental Replay

This tool was inspired by Stagen's Performance Journaling tool "Gamefilming." Stagen's tool was based on various resources including:

Argyris, Chris. *Overcoming Organizational Defenses.* Allyn & Bacon, 1990.

Senge, Peter. *The Fifth Discipline.* Currency, 1990.

Stone, Douglas. Patton, Bruce. & Heen, Sheila. *Difficult Conversations: How to Discuss What Matters Most.* Penguin Books, 1999.

Womeldorff, David. *The Power of TED: The Empowerment Dynamic.* Polaris, 2005.

Pause Points

Jones, Mark. *Be With Jesus 365.*

Reflection/Questioning

Sinclair, Tracy. *Reflective Practice.* Coach Advancement.

Chapter 7: Project

Gap Analysis

Original practice, developed through trial-and-error.

Chapter 8: Practice Small

3-30-90

Credit for the inspiration of this practice goes to a former student and global learning and development manager at a global financial services firm.

Think big/practice small
"9 Strategies to Think Big and Work Small." Product HQ, 2024.

Chapter 9: Measure Progress

I am/I Will Statements
Graham, Ashley. *The Power of "I AM" Statements.* Linkedin, 2023.
Groeschel, Craig. "The Power to Change Your Habits: Identity Drives Behavior." YouTube, 2023.

Measure Progress
"How To Measure Your Progress Effectively in 5 Steps." Indeed, 2024.

Chapter 10: Practice Accountability

Accountability Partners
"5C's of Effective Accountability Partners." ITD World.

Brand Development Tracker
Cote, Catherine. *Personal Branding: What It Is & Why It Matters.* Harvard Business School, 2024.

Chapter 12: Maximize Life Outside the 10%

70-20-10 model
"Achieving 100 Percent of the 70-20-10 Leadership Development Model Using Business Simulations." Association for Talent Development, 2018.

Chapter 13: D.I.Y. & Grow Others

Modeling
"Observational Learning (Modeling)." OpenStax, 2014.

Social learning
Bandura, Albert. *Social Learning Theory.* General learning Corporation, 1971.

APPENDIX B

Leader Lessons

To gain some outside perspective and insights on leadership and authentic leader development, I had a small team of researchers interview leaders from various sectors across multiple industries. We interviewed 19 leaders from nonprofit, for-profit, governmental, and education sectors. These men and women come from a swath of industries including healthcare, retail, automotive, financial, cybersecurity, corporate services, and church ministry.

Below are key lessons they shared, organized topically and sub-topically. Their names are omitted to protect their confidentiality, but I've listed their level, sector, and/or industry. You'll also find chapter cross references in case you'd like to further apply their lessons to the content, tips, and techniques in the book. Enjoy their lessons and words of wisdom on a variety of topics!

Accountability & Commitment

Commitment, Being All In on Leadership Development

- Leadership development, you have to want it and be open. Nobody's gonna go through a program and become a leader unless they're all in. So, it's how much you're open to receive it and reflect and dive in. And not multitask, not go through to check the box like that will never develop you. It has to be about immersing yourself into it. (Vice President, Healthcare) (Chapter 2)

Other-Accountability & Getting Feedback

- So there's just some very basic, rudimentary, you just have to practice but it starts with having an awareness. Okay, I've got some I've got some weaknesses, and I need to work on those weaknesses if I'm going to be a better leader. Yeah, I've got somebody to help me in hopefully a gracious and non-threatening way, point those things out and work on them. (President & CEO, Nonprofit, Healthcare) (Chapter 10, Chapter 12, Chapter 13)

Practicing Self-Accountability

- Journaling has been huge for me. And so like, every day I journal, I start with gratitude. I usually try to write at least five things that I'm grateful for. And then I dive into just an authentic prayer before God and sometimes those things are things that are just between me and him… And so I think that constant, bringing myself before God, bringing myself into those moments to one, be vulnerable before him, actually creates opportunities for me to be vulnerable for other people. (Senior Pastor) (Chapter 10)

Adaptation

Using Feedback to Grow

- I would get a counselor. Yeah, a therapist or a counselor. I mean, if you're going to therapy and counseling or life coaching or whatever you want to call it you're learning more about yourself and learning how to live with other people and I mean, it's going to manifest in your business. You know, I have a great time when I meet with my therapist. He calls out my BS and encourages me and when I'm scratching my head, he has tools and ideas. (Market Leader, Systems Integration & Cybersecurity) (Chapter 12)

- I'll do what I call seatbelt sessions with my team. Just as you can imagine when you strap on a seatbelt or require them to give me one piece of feedback that I have, that I'm asking them to give me and I don't have any feedback for you is not an option. Okay? It has to be something even if it's something you think I'm okay yet, you think that maybe I can do better. And it's called seatbelt sessions. And that's for me to grow, to make sure that my intent is actually being carried out. (Director, Development, Government) (Chapter 12)

Authenticity and Development

Authenticity, Authentic Leadership:

- Someone that is transparent and honest, that has earned the trust of the people that they're leading. I would say that would be an authentic leader. Just knowing that the people that report to you know that you have their back and you also expect them to be trustworthy and honest with you also. (Director, Nonprofit, Healthcare) (Chapter 3, Chapter 5)

- An authentic leader is a leader that is driven by relationship. In my opinion. You can't be authentic without a relationship. Leadership…doesn't even include mandate and rules or structure. Leadership, really, at its core level was influence. And it's up to that leader whether that influence is positive or negative. (Owner & Director, Nonprofit, Healthcare) (Chapter 5)

- As a leader, you have to be willing to change and, and that will allow your authenticity to come out too because your team then sees, hey, he recognized that we weren't going in the right direction. (Senior Advisor, Financial Services) (Chapter 5)

- If you want to go kind of biblical, let your yes be yes or no be no. Or another way to put it is just say what you mean and mean what you say. Just being a person of your word and being a person of honor and there's a lot that goes into that. (President & CEO, Nonprofit, Healthcare) (Chapter 5)

- I think really being authentic is trying to figure out what type of leader you are, whether it's a servant leader, whether it's a very prescriptive leader versus all the other types of leaders that are out there. And then showing that to people, because ultimately, if people find out that you're fake and how you are portraying yourself isn't matching reality. They'll lose all trust in you as a leader, and you'll come across very negatively as this hypocrite more than anything else. (C-Suite Leader, Information Technology) (Chapter 5)

Formal & Informal Development

- The development is beyond the formal right why while I provide a lot of formal development programs, and I tell the participants to this way, when I'm exposed to a new thing, for example, that's development, right when my leader asks me like, Hey, have you had experience on this? Well, not really well, this is a good development. Opportunity, right? Being really open and ready to take on maybe stretch assignments in the not in not outside of traditional classroom setting is a development and I get, I get that a lot. (Senior Manager, Talent & Organization Development) (Chapter 1)

Connection & Collaboration

Learning Together, Forming a Practice Team

- You can have a culture on your team. It could be three to five people; you could have a culture. For me, it's a practice group. I lead a group of about 20 people. And I tried to, I learned through some of the leadership stuff I went before if I can have a really strong culture with my teammates, and for me, that means a couple things. (Managing Partner, Public Relations) (Chapter 13)

Listening, Authenticity, & Connecting with People

- I think listening as a leader is tied pretty strongly to authenticity. To the better listeners, in general, I think will be the better leaders for the next segment of life just in terms of how society shaped and that's hard, because there is for some reason this this attachment of speaking and being heard and leadership and how they have to be connected and I think that goes against the norm to say hey, I want to be a listener I want the words that I do speak to have power because I'm not always talking. (Associate Athletic Director, University) (Chapter 6)

Transferring Leadership Development Back to your Job; Sharing with Others

- Some of it is just more about reflection. It's about reflecting and then the other thing, which I think is really important is sharing. Yeah. What I mean by that is I've told my team, my direct leaders, hey, here's what I learned. (C-Suite Leader, Vice President, Information Technology) (Chapter 6, Chapter 12, Chapter 13)

- Anytime I go to any professional learning, development, read a book, or just learn something from a journal. My next team meeting we will discuss it, okay? So, I always share with them what I learned how that applies to our work as a team, and how we can use this to, you know, move the needle, if you will, in our line of work. (Director, Development, Government) (Chapter 12, Chapter 13)

Continuous Learning & Growth

Being a Lifelong Learner

- I think you have to understand that if you're not willing to change, change is gonna run over you. And leave tire tracks on the back. Frankly, the job is more interesting if you commit to being a lifelong learner. See the changes and understand them and embrace them so you don't get left behind. (Managing Partner, Public Relations) (Chapter 5)

How to Make Learning Stick

- Practice, practice, practice, right? A lot of people you and I including myself, go to the library and read a book or download a book on Audible or go to a weekend training or to a workshop. It's great, right? Some of them are super engaging the last takeaways, and then Monday rolls around and you're back to school at work. And it just goes in the file cabinet somewhere in a notebook. You don't apply it right. (Owner, Business & Executive Coaching) (Chapter 8)

Learning from Challenges & Pain Points

- Our director of sales and sponsorship left in November...it was a great learning experience for me...I learned a lot about some of our sponsors, learned a lot about some of the pain points at that position probably feels, and I think the takeaways for me are I need to do a few different things... and I could do myself a favor by learning a few things now and being in the know a little bit better...I've got to figure out a way to take this off this person's plate or how can we be more efficient with this? (Associate Athletic Director, University) (Chapter 5)

Learning from Role Models while Being Authentic

- I think the most important thing that's really important is there's a lot of people that you can look up to who are fantastic leaders. And they're different from you. And so, a lot of times you're like, I'm gonna be just like him and do this. And that's not your authentic self. Yeah. It doesn't mean you can't use some of the things they do and allow that to be better. But realize that everybody is different and has different things they bring to the table for a reason. (C-Suite Leader, Information Technology) (Chapter 13)

Overcoming Barriers to Learning and Continuous Growth

- Some people just don't want to change. They think they know it all. They think of the smartest person in the room pride. They think they're better than everybody else on this, you know, and those people so the two words "I know," are the two most power-ful words in the English language that stop learning. Because the very second that you think or say that your brain shuts off you don't you stop listening. So, we've actually watched those two words, right, we can replace those with isn't that interesting? Tell me more about that … (Owner, Business & Executive Coaching) (Chapter 2)

Curiosity & Open-Mindedness

Being Curious, Open about your Development

- A key principle is curiosity. It's not a blueprint. It's an exploration. This is being outside in the wilderness, seeing a far-off mountaintop and thinking I want to get there. I don't totally know how I'm going to get there. But I can see my next step. I'm going this way on the path, and I'm committed to doing it. And then when I get to a fork in the road, I'm going to look back up and see shoot, I still want to go out that mountain. I don't know if I'm going the right way or…I'm going to be curious enough at each moment in time to dig in and realize I don't have to have the answers, but I'm here to explore here to find the answers. (Vice President, Training & Development, Retail) (Chapter 2)

Learning from Practice & Observation

- Some of development is all about trial and error, right? And you figure out what works and maybe what doesn't work just in how you go about your interactions with other people. But for me, I think I learned by watching. (Associate Athletic Director, University) (Chapter 8, Chapter 13)

Practical Application & Change

Intentionality & Implementing Changes

- It's…truly just doing the work to understand who you want to be, what are your opportunities and in being really tactical about how you're going to implement them and then making sure that you're conscious about doing that, because it's easy to just go right back in, you know, to the way that you always do things and yeah, so there's definitely some major intentionality there. (Senior Manager, Corporate Communications, Retail) (Chapter 3)

Learning through Repetition, Measuring Progress

- If it's a habit, I'm trying to change, because we're human, it's easy to fall right back into routines. And oftentimes, you don't even realize you're not following your new program or your new habit building until it becomes a problem. You're visiting it again. Well, I tried to stay mindful of that throughout the day. I'm not going to lie and say I looked at it every day, but I tried to remind myself once in a while of things I'm trying to change so I don't really have to revisit these things that way again, so I think that's all it is, is repetition. (Director, Development, Government) (Chapter 9)

- The key is learning different strategies and concepts, leadership development, and putting them into action, test and measure, you know, we can test, and we can tie some things down to like measurables here so that we know what's working. What isn't. It's easier to stop what isn't working and keep doing what is working. So that's another aspect of what I do is try and break things down. Where do you want to go? What are the goals and results that you want? And then what are the steps we think we can take to get there…We're going to test and measure and then I can hold them accountable. When you said you were going to do this and this and that, but you didn't. Why not? What got in the way? (Owner, Business & Executive Coaching) (Chapter 9)

Practicing Small

- It kind of comes down to you gotta pick to my point about like, what if you're writing a value statement or whatever, like, how do you want others to see you like, what are those things and then what are comparing that to like, where you want to go and like things you might need or whatever, pick one or two things because you're not going to change 50 things. (Senior Manager, Corporate Communications, Retail) (Chapter 8, Chapter 10)

- I think one piece is don't bite off more than you can chew. It's that whole saying "Rome wasn't built in a day." You do not need to you may have goals or you may have ideals, things that you want to be true. You don't need to do them all today. You really don't just get one and do that one. Like just do that one thing.

Figure out what that one thing is and do it. And then once it's become part of your habit, like part of your natural tendency. (Vice President, Training & Development, Retail) (Chapter 8, Chapter 10)

Self-Awareness & Reflection

Identifying Your *Why?*

- Children are, in my estimation, one of the great, greatest leadership teaching tools you'll encounter. When I go home, my son or daughter couldn't care less what title I have. Yeah, they don't see me as vice president. You know, they see me as dad and what are we going to do with the family? Everybody that has children has the opportunity to be a great leader and to practice leadership. (C-Suite Leader, Vice President, Information Technology) (Chapter 5)

Projecting–what do I want to work on, who do I want to become?

- What I have done is I've been very intentional about, what are the other developments that I'm getting, and I am surgical about this, and I am intentional about them...I think it needs to be something that you're genuinely interested in...when it's something that you would be really interested in and see value in, that feels very authentic to me. (Global Director, Leader Development) (Chapter 7)

Reflecting & Taking a Pause

- The most important step and how I reflect it is that I take a breath first. If I don't take the breath first and I immediately start speaking probably like eight out of 10 times I end up having to change the trajectory of where we're going. If I take the breath, it gives me the moment to figure it out. Also, I typically do 30 minutes where before I lay down and go to sleep, I think through the decisions I had to make through the day. And I just figured out Hey, how did I handle that one? Was that appropriate? (Senior Advisor, Financial Services) (Chapter 6)

Vulnerability & Humility

- I think when people become a "leader," which for most people, it just means you've been given a title, given influence, the first thing that needs to come with influence is to understand, yes, I may have been given influence, but I still don't have all the answers…I don't have it all together. But I'm willing to learn, I'm willing to grow. There's a humility of truly admitting…I don't have every single answer to everybody's question, especially in leadership. (Senior Pastor) (Chapter 4)

- Being vulnerable means that maybe when you are not at your best anymore, sometimes exposing yourself means Oh, in order to be functioning at my best I need to tell you that I'm not at my best right now. (Senior Manager, Talent & Organization Development) (Chapter 4)

- I am open and honest. Maybe to a fault. A sensitive leader, I think that sometimes maybe people could see that as somebody that you can walk on or push around because they're not as rigid or tough. Hardline as other leaders that people have. I'm aware of that though. I will say like, it can present challenges, but for me, you also have to be aware of yourself. And so if you're, if you understand your own personality and your personality traits, your own style, you're going to realize that that's an area that could be vulnerable for you…I have to be aware that if somebody, for example, came from a leader that was like that, and then they are working with me, they could potentially think that they could, you know, walk over me or push me and I'm aware of that. (Managing Partner, Public Relations) (Chapter 4)

About Dr. Fyke

Dr. Jeremy Fyke is a Nashville-based professor, leader developer, and business owner. He has a Ph.D. in Organizational Communication from Purdue University. Dr. Fyke is a "PracAdemic" who's passionate about bringing the corporate and university worlds together. He's an associate professor in Communication Studies and Director of Character-Centered Leadership at Belmont University, where he oversees leadership development for all employees across campus. His research interests include leadership, organizational learning and development, leadership coaching, and organizational culture. Outside Belmont, he operates Authentic Leader Development, a talent development and leadership coaching company. In late 2020, Dr. Fyke also founded Two Heads Hot Sauce, a gourmet sauce and spice company he sold in 2024 that still operates today. He lives outside Nashville, Tennessee with his wife, Brooke, and two daughters, Emma and Lennon. Dr. Fyke's purpose is to use all the opportunities and platforms he's given to bless others and glorify God in everything he does.

How to Stay in Touch With Me

Thank you for getting a copy of *Have We Met? Discovering the Authentic Leader You Never Knew*. I pray that this book has impacted you in multiple ways. If it has, I'd love to hear from you. Reach out to me by email. Share your wins and takeaways on LinkedIn, tag me, and use the hashtag #HaveWeMet.

Secondly, what you read here is only a snapshot of the work my team and I get to do on a regular basis. We'd love to connect further and help your team whether it's through seminars and workshops, one-on-one or group coaching, or our consulting services for your organization.

Let's stay connected and keep the conversation going!
God bless,

Jeremy

jeremyfyke@gmail.com
www.AuthenticLeaderDevelopment.com

About Authentic Leader Development

Authentic Leader Development exists to help leaders and teams discover, develop, and apply their authentic leadership voice to communicate effectively and get results. Dr. Fyke brings his unique blend of academic knowledge, industry experience, and passion to help you develop and drive results.

As a sought-after speaker and facilitator, Dr. Fyke has been training, coaching, and consulting with leaders at all levels, from companies of all sizes and industries, including healthcare, manufacturing, retail, government, banking, and professional communications.

Whether you're looking for a keynote speaker for your corporate conference, a facilitator for your offsite retreat, or a partner to coach your executives one-on-one, Dr. Fyke and his team are ready to come alongside you every step of the way.

www.ingramcontent.com/pod-product-compliance
Lightning Source LLC
Chambersburg PA
CBHW060135130626
46556CB00006B/2359